WILLIAM
SHAKESPEARE'S
THE TAMING
OF THE
CLUELESS

WILLIAM SHAKESPEARE'S

The Taming of the Clueless

BY IAN DOESCHER

INSPIRED BY THE WORK OF
Amy Heckerling AND
William Shakespeare

QUIRK BOOKS
PHILADELPHIA

For family, in broad and narrow senses—
To Jennifer, Graham, Liam, J, and T—
For giving me your patience and your love
Especially in times when I was clueless

A Pop Shakespeare Book

Clueless

TM & © 2020 Paramount Pictures. All Rights Reserved.

Library of Congress Cataloging-in-Publication Data
Doescher, Ian, author. | Barton, Kent, illustrator. | Green, Helen, cover artist
Taming of the clueless / by Ian Doescher ; interior illustrations by Kent
Barton ; cover illustration by Helen Green.
LCSH: Shakespeare, William, 1564–1616—Parodies, imitations, etc. |
Clueless (Motion picture)—Adaptations.
PS3604.O3419 T36 2020
DDC 812/.6—dc23   2019038539

ISBN: 978-1-68369-175-4

Printed in Canada

Typeset in Sabon

Text by Ian Doescher
Cover designed by Andie Reid
Interior designed by Molly Rose Murphy
Interior illustrations by Kent Barton
Cover illustration by Helen Green
Production management by John J. McGurk

Quirk Books
215 Church Street
Philadelphia, PA 19106
quirkbooks.com

10 9 8 7 6 5 4 3 2 1

A NOTE ABOUT THE SERIES

Welcome to the world of Pop Shakespeare!

Each book in this series gives a Shakespearean makeover to your favorite movie or television show, re-creating each moment from the original as if the Bard of Avon had written it himself. The lines are composed in iambic pentameter, and the whole is structured into acts and scenes, complete with numbered lines and stage directions.

Astute readers will be delighted to discover Easter eggs, historical references, and sly allusions to Shakespeare's most famous plays, characters, and themes, which you can learn more about in the author's Afterword. A Reader's Guide is also included, for those who want to learn more about Shakespeare's style.

LIST OF ILLUSTRATIONS

DRAMATIS PERSONAE

CHER, *a young woman*

DIONNE, *her friend*

TAI, *Cher's protégé*

JOSH, *Cher's ex-stepbrother*

MURRAY, *Dionne's paramour*

TRAVIS, *a layabout*

ELTON, *a brute*

CHRISTIAN, *a fop*

AMBER, *a bitter young woman*

SUMMER *and* LAWRENCE, *students*

HEATHER, *Josh's sometime paramour*

MEL HOROWITZ, *Cher's father*

LADY TOBY GEIST, *a schoolmarm*

MASTER WENDELL HALL, *a scholar*

LUCY, *a cleaning woman*

LADY STOEGER, *a physical education teacher*

GAIL, *Josh's mother*

BALTHASAR, *a musician*

JANE, *a narrator*

VARIOUS PUPILS *and* INSTRUCTORS

PROLOGUE

Beverly Hills, California, in the New World.

Enter JANE, *a narrator.*

JANE   Cher—handsome, clever, rich—who had a home
Most comfortable, a happy disposition,
Seem'd to unite, wherever she did roam,
The blessings of existence's condition.
She lived for some untrammel'd sixteen years   5
Within the world, with little to distress
Or vex her. Nothing brought her unto tears—
Though on herself she could have ponder'd less.
Her father treated her indulgently—
Cher's mother died too long ago for her   10
To have any distinctive memory
Of the caresses she did once confer.
Behold what challenges to Cher arrive—
The romance of a virgin who can't drive.

                                         [Exit.

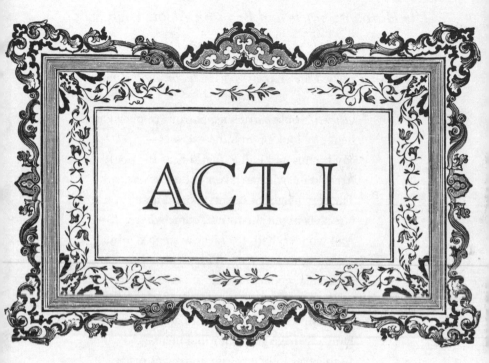

ACT I

SCENE 1

The Horowitz house and Bronson Alcott High School.

Enter CHER, DIONNE, MURRAY, AMBER, *and other* STUDENTS
at a party. Enter BALTHASAR *aside, providing music.*

CHER   [*aside:*] Noble patricians, patrons of my right,
            Belike ye look upon mine excesses—
            My friends and I all gather'd near the pool,
            Array'd in swimsuits, sun upon our backs,
            The very height of beauty, youth, and joy,   5
            No cares about the future, come what will—
            And wonder: hath I somehow stepp'd inside
            A strange advertisement for cleansing cream?
            Noxzema, goddess Greek of lasses pure,
            Hath no role in the drama that we play.   10
            Take mine assurance—nobles, groundlings both—
            I am a teenage girl of normal life,
            Who never look'd to rise above her place
            Or face the world with aught but normalcy.

BALTHASAR   [*singing:*] Behold, beyond the window, 'neath the sky,   15
            The rushing carriages do pass thee by,
            Whilst I do sit, to loneliness resign'd,
            And ponder wherefore questions fill my mind.
            'Tis Friday night! I feel the soothing heat
            And search this filthy city for a beat—   20
                Downtown, the young ones go, hey nonny non,
                Downtown, the young ones grow, hey nonny hey!
                We are the children of America,

The children we of new America.

[Exeunt all but Cher.

CHER   My days are spent, I'll wager, as yours are—   25
Each morn I rise with brushing of the teeth,
And choose my clothing for the day to come.
So many dresses, doublets, pantaloons,
Vests, girdles, hoop skirts, blouses, hose, and shoes—
In combinations of the rainbow's hues—   30
That I must use a system most advanc'd
To tell me whether what I did select
Displays a fashion sense befitting of
My reputation as a lady fine.
Once I am satisfied my garments shall   35

Give complement unto my disposition,
I am prepar'd to say good morning to
My father, Mel, a litigator he.
His are the most ferocious types of lawyers—
He chargeth forth with lawsuits like a knight   40
And storms ten castles ere the noon bell rings.
Our cleaning woman, Lucy, fears his strength,
And rushes from him when he entereth.
So skill'd my father is that he may charge
Five hundred ducats should he choose to grant   45
His talent, voice, and wisdom to your suit.
'Tis privilege to know the mighty man,
And better yet to be his only daughter.
He fighteth like a pugilist against
His enemies across the courtroom floor—   50
Yet though so many pay him for the honor,
He fighteth me for free, no charge requir'd,
For I am daughter to the mighty Mel.

Enter MEL HOROWITZ. CHER *hands him a glass of juice.*

MEL   O, shall it ever be this juice with thee?
CHER   The vitamins the earth provides are vital   55
        If thou wouldst healthy be and healthy stay.
        A for thy teeth, thy bones, and tissue soft,
        B6 to keep thy brain in proper function,
        B12 for central nervous system health,
        C—in this juice—for gums and healing pow'r,   60
        D that thou mayst have calcium in full,
        E for thy red blood cells to form and thrive,
        K for coagulation of the blood.

	An alphabet of wonders natural
	That none but fools and scoundrels would disdain. 65
	Thou wouldst be none of these methinks, 'tis true?
MEL	Where is my satchel? I am late to leave.
CHER	Two months hath pass'd since we to Malibu
	Have ventur'd. Father, now the time hath come.
MEL	Did those two droning dismal-dreaming knaves 70
	Call on thee once again?
CHER	—They are thy parents,
	And thou dost owe them some allegiance, sir.
	They have begot thee, bred thee, lov'd thee; thou
	Return those duties back as are right fit:
	Obey them, love them, and most honor them. 75
	Today, thou must not slither from thine office
	Like serpents in the grass avoiding hawks.
	Good Doctor Lovett shall convene with thee—
	He hath consulted with th'apothecary
	And shall dispense thine influenza shot. 80
MEL	One shot unwelcome doth deserve another:
	My stepson Josh shall sup with us tonight.
CHER	Yet why?
MEL	—He is stepbrother unto thee.
CHER	Thou wert but married to his mum a trice
	Ere ye were justifiably divorc'd, 85
	Yet Josh hangs on like barnacle to rock.
	'Twas five years hence, a length of time too long
	For him to still pursue a link with thee.
	Say wherefore, then, must I spend time withal?
MEL	Divorce is made for spouses, not for children. 90
CHER	Take thou thy juice and I'll consider it.
MEL	Forget thy juice, and thou shalt still do so.

                                                          [Exit Mel.

CHER   *[aside:]* He is a man of wondrous temper, yea,
            Yet also sparks of generosity.
            Did I yet show to ye the carriage he   95
            Hath giv'n to me upon my birthday last?
                              *[She reveals her carriage, climbs
                                    into it, and begins driving.*
            In faith, this coach is loqu'd out in the height.
            Four wheels that do propel the cart along,
            Bags fill'd with air for safety on each side,
            A music box that traveleth beside   100
            As if an orchestra did with thee ride.
            No license have I thus to operate,
            Yet 'tis a learning vehicle, no more.
            The neighbors' statuettes and planting boxes
            Athwart my passage stand at their own risk—   105
            When Cher doth hold the reins behind the wheel,
            Whate'er is not affix'd unto the earth
            May be in peril grave, I do confess.
            Arrive I presently to Dionne's home—
            My closest friend and ally, verily.   110
            We have in common much, yet mainly this:
            The jealousy of many touches us—
            We know what 'tis to face the green-ey'd monster.
            Dionne and I were christen'd after two
            Fantastic singers of a bygone time,   115
            Who—in the present time—hath found their fame
            Upon the stages of the infomercials.

            Enter DIONNE, *climbing into* CHER'*s carriage.*

DIONNE   Holla, sweet Cher.

CHER   —My best, my darling mate!
I must remark upon thy bravery
That thou wouldst wear such frippery as this.   120
Thou ever hadst courageous fashion efforts.

DIONNE   Thou likest, then, my hat?

CHER   —Did Doctor Seuss
Take thee unto a haberdashery,
And afterward treat thee unto a meal
Of em'rald chicken's eggs and *jambon vert*?   125

DIONNE   Perhaps 'tis not the fashion of the day,
Yet I—unlike thee, dear—skinn'd not a collie
To fabricate a handbag.

CHER   —'Tis faux collie.
                I prithee, dog me not with mockery.
DIONNE   Didst see? Thou pass'd a sign that bid thee stop—   130
                'Twas large and red, octagonally shap'd—
                Yet thou drove on like thou wert being chas'd.
CHER   A pause complete I register'd therein.
DIONNE   If thou shalt thus maintain, I'll not gainsay,
                So loyal is my friendship unto thee.   135

                          *[They arrive at their school. A bell
                                    rings to summon Dionne.*

                Eight-thirty on the instant and the ring
                Of Murray's summons plays upon mine ears.
                The lad's love for me riseth with the sun.

                Enter various STUDENTS *swirling around them.*

CHER   Belike he'd gladly make thee his possession,
                A gunnysack to carry by his side.   140
DIONNE   Thou hast it right—this weekend he did call
                Upon me, asking, "Whither art thou bound,
                And where hast been these several past hours?"
                Responded I, "At my grandmother's house,
                Where o'er the river, through the woods I went—"   145
CHER   [*aside:*] 'Tis ever thus with Dionne and her Murray—
                The lovers e'er enact a drama vast,
                As if they were but actors on a stage,
                Their scenes with rage, desire, and passion writ,
                The world their audience, which hangs upon   150
                Each angry, tender word the players speak.
                Not since the households of Verona hath
                There been a tale of paramours as these.

> Belike they have too frequently observ'd
> The tale of Tina Turner and her Ike.   155
> Yet what's love got to do with it? Speak not,
> 'Tis but my part to ask this question next:
> [*To Dionne:*] Dee, wherefore dost thou bear the horrid
>   boy,
> For thou 'mongst women art a paragon
> And could choose any lad thou dost desire.   160

DIONNE   Tut! He approacheth suddenly.

                    Enter MURRAY.

MURRAY   —My lass,
> Why answerest thou not my many bells?
> More times I rang for thee to hither come
> Than old Westminster Abbey chimes each day.

DIONNE   Call me not lass if thou wouldst answer'd be.   165
>   *[Students gather to hear
>   Dionne and Murray argue.*

MURRAY   Where wert thou all the livelong weekend, dear?
> My fear doth grow that thou dost jump the jeep
> With someone else and cuckold makest me.

DIONNE   "Dost jump the jeep"? What newfound words are
>   these?

MURRAY   Thou knowest well the meaning of the phrase.   170

DIONNE   If thou wouldst speak of sex upon four wheels,
> Perchance thou wilt address another matter:
> How did this hair extension—from a mart
> Whose worthlessness is known e'en by the simple—
> Appear within thy carriage's back seat?   175

MURRAY   Nay, ask me not. It seemeth that the strand

	Is one of thy thin locks, spaghetti-like,

Is one of thy thin locks, spaghetti-like,
Which e'er adorn the pasta of thy pate.

DIONNE No cheap, substandard hair hath ever touch'd
    The fashionable head of Dionne, lout!   180
    It, peradventure, cometh from Shawanna—
    She wanna find her way inside thy trousers!

CHER Dee, I must fly, for class begins anon!

              [Cher walks on.

DIONNE Farewell!
MURRAY   —Why wouldst thou—
DIONNE   —Nay, we two are done.
    Like Anne Boleyn, there's naught for us ahead. 185

MURRAY Mayhap the red moon rises over thee,
    And thou art in thy menses once again?

              [All students gasp.

DIONNE O, villain of unpardonable speech!

      [Exeunt Dionne and Murray, arguing.

CHER *[aside:]* In sooth, I know not wherefore Dionne doth
    Spend all her courting time with high school lads. 190
    They are like dogs, ill-manner'd and uncouth,
    Which one must ever clean and feed and train—
    Such nervous creatures, slobbering about
    And leaving stains upon thy garments best.

          [A boy approaches Cher and
             puts his arm around her.

    [To boy:] Off, brute! Or I shall cage thee. *[Aside:]* Fie,
                as if! 195

    As if he should so blatantly approach,
    As if I would, then, fall into his arms,
    As if we two familiar would become,
    As if he could usurp my maidenhood!

CHER *walks into class with other* STUDENTS,
including MURRAY, TRAVIS, ELTON, *and* AMBER.
Enter MASTER WENDELL HALL, *teaching.*

HALL   The question of our time today is this: 200
              Should all oppressèd people of the world
              Be given refuge in America?
              Is't inconceivable, or justified?
              First Amber, thou shalt take the stance against,
              And Cher, thou speakest in defense thereof.   205
              Thou hast two minutes, Cher—I bid thee, speak.

CHER   'Tis well, 'tis passing simple, take ye heed:
              The Haiti-ites must to America
              An they would safe be from their government,
              Yet some would argue—mayhap Amber shall—   210
              'Tis far too great a strain on our resources.
              I think upon a garden party, which
              For my dear father I did lately hold—
              Répondez, s'il vous plaît was my request,
              Since 'twas a formal dinner I arrang'd.   215
              Still, some arriv'd who did *répondez* not,
              Which was discourteous in the extreme.
              My mind was vex'd by unexpected guests—
              Rush'd I unto the kitchen hastily,
              Did redistribute food upon the trenchers,   220
              And added table settings in a trice.
              Though there was much of Sturm und Drang that day,
              "The more the merrier!" was soon the cry.
              All's well that ends well, as the maxim goes.
              Ye see, then, the conclusion of my case: 225
              If but our government hied to the kitchen,

And swiftly rearrang'd the meals therein,
Our party could include the Haiti-ites
And all would have enow to celebrate.
To finish, this reminder would I give: 230
It sayeth not *répondez, s'il vous plaît*
Upon the Statue of our Liberty!
          [Students applaud.
My thanks—my case doth rest upon this point.

HALL   Now, Amber, 'tis the time for thy reply.

AMBER   Yet, Master Hall, how should this answer'd be?   235
The topic should be Haiti, yet she speaks
Of parties, meals, and guests. 'Tis nonsense, yea?

CHER   His birthday fiftieth th'occasion was,
Not just a random merriment.
      [Amber holds her fingers up to form a W.

AMBER   —Whate'er.
If Cher shall not proceed as 'twas assign'd,   240
I cannot treat the matter earnestly.

HALL   Ye may be seated, then. Do any here
Have further thoughts upon th'oration that
Cher hath presented? Elton, pond'rest thou?

ELTON   My thought is this: I am at pains to find   245
The music program of the Cranberries
That once was here, within my trusty bag.
I must unto the quad, ere it is ta'en.

HALL   Alas, such wandering I'll not permit.
What further insights from ye scholars young?   250

TRAVIS   Insights aplenty enter my mind.

HALL   I wait with bated breath upon thy thoughts.

TRAVIS   What I think of the Rolling Stones, sir,
Is how of Nine Inch Nails my children

	Shall think—someday, when I have children,	255
	My mother I should, then, not torment.	
HALL	Indeed! Thou art far gone from Haiti, Travis,	
	Yet tolerance is e'er a lesson that	
	Is worthy of the learning, by my troth—	
	E'en when the subject out of nowhere comes.	260
	To speak of nowhere—which is, verily,	
	Where some of ye are headed in your lives—	
	The time hath come, report cards to distribute.	
	Shall ye find A thereon? Astounding work.	
	Perhaps a B? 'Tis Blameless, utterly.	265
	If you spy C, thou hast a Common grade,	

	Whereas a D is Difficult indeed.	
	Yet if ye see an F, you have Fail'd me—	
	Not only me, nay, also fail'd yourselves.	
	Is there a Christian Stovitz in this class?	270
CHER	Reports of Christian tell us, Master Hall,	

CHER   Reports of Christian tell us, Master Hall,
              His parents share joint custody o'er him.
              He shall, then, split his time in school in twain—
              The first semester in Chicagoland,
              The second here. To me, the matter's plain: 275
              A tragedy of our professional legal.

HALL   My thanks for thine astute perspective, Cher.
                        [Master Hall passes report cards
                              to students in the front row, who
                              disseminate them throughout the class.

TRAVIS   [*aside:*] Alas, how shall my parents bellow!

HALL   Your conversations, prithee, set aside.
                              [Travis prepares to jump out
                                    the window in dismay.

TRAVIS   [*aside:*] O, moment dire! I'll ope the window,   280
              And sleep—and by sleep to say we end
              The horrid grades our work is heir to.

HALL   Desist with all your suicide attempts—
              I ne'er have lost a student over grades
              And do not plan to start the trend today.   285
              If ye would shuffle off this mortal coil,
              You must postpone 'til second period.
                              [He pulls Travis back inside.

CHER   [*aside:*] Bleak darkness gathers o'er my sunny day
              And swarms into first period like gnats
              That cloud the firmament with fearful portent.   290
              What change the weather brings, for I've receiv'd

A grade of C in my debate class—fie,
'Tis Cruel, Callous, Critical, and Crude!

The bell rings. All disperse.
Enter DIONNE *walking with* CHER.

O, Dee, hast thou thine own report card got?

DIONNE   Indeed, and I shall pay the price for it,   295
As if I were the bread, my grades the pyre,
And quickly I'll be toasted in the flames.

CHER   I chok'd as though a bone lodg'd in my throat.
My father, soon enow, shall see my grade
And like a missile shall ballistic go!   300

DIONNE   The grades of Master Hall were passing harsh—
What drives a man to treat his students so?
My grade was C, by minus punctuated.

CHER   Mine C, which pulls my av'rage swiftly down.

DIONNE   What shall we do?

CHER   —Some plan we must conceive.   305
Pray, think on it awhile and we shall speak—
Injustice such as this must answer'd be.
                    [Exeunt all except Dionne.

DIONNE   C minus, ah! 'Tis passing negative,
Why minus? Tiny line that shakes one's soul,
Ah, minus! Students wince—this doth define us,   310
O, wherefore do I have a wretched minus?
                    [Exit.

SCENE 2

The Horowitz house.

Enter CHER, *near a portrait of her mother.*

CHER   My house, is't not a classic of design?
        The columns are from fifteen ninety-two,
        Near prehistoric, by my reckoning.
        Behold the portrait of my mother dear,
        A betty of a beauty, who hath died   5
        When I was but an infant newly born—
        Some accident of fate befell her whilst
        She underwent postpartum liposuction.
        No memories have I of her, alas,
        Yet still pretend she watcheth over me.   10
        [*To portrait:*] Superb marks earn'd I in geometry,
        Art thou not proud thereof, sweet mother mine?
        Yet, what is this my senses do receive—
        What strains are these that echo in mine ears,
        Play'd by a music box of somber tone?   15
        The maudlin melodies of college tunes,
        The universally sad harmonies
        Resounding through our universities—
        These can mean but one thing: Josh hath arriv'd.

        Enter JOSH, *looking into the ice house.*

        Canst tell me wherefore thou wouldst listen to   20
        Such ballads as would make a strong man cry?

JOSH   Holla, my halfway sister. Thou art here,
              So who then watcheth o'er the Galleria,
              Where thou dost ever spend thy precious time?

CHER   Thy shirt of flannel—dost thou pay respect   25
              Unto the gods who make Seattle gray,
              Or merely, mayhap, needest thou the warmth
              Because thou near the ice house ever stand'st?
                                        [He pokes her side.

JOSH   Thy belly filleth like a burlap sack.

CHER   Thy face doth race to catch up with thy mouth,   30
              For both are filthy.

JOSH   —If thou wouldst face truth,
              Thy tongue is far too sharp to match thy mien.

CHER   Thy face too mean for me to hold my tongue.

JOSH   Thy sharpness tells a tale a man could fear.

CHER   Thy tongue and face should turn their tails and flee.   35

JOSH   A flea would gladly take a turn on thee.

CHER   Thy tongue dost turn its face to tales. Farewell.

JOSH   With my tongue in your tail? Let us restart.
              I visited with Father at his office.

CHER   The man is not thy father; wherefore canst   40
              Thou not some other fam'ly find to torture?

JOSH   My mother may have married someone else,
              Yet this makes th'other man no father mine.

CHER   Indeed, such is the meaning of the word—
              What is a father but thy mother's love?   45
              Thou turnest words so that their sense doth flee—
              I prithee, stay not at our house too long.

JOSH   With such a welcome, surely 'tis my hope,
              For who'd not bask in sunshine such as thou
              Hast, in these moments, shone upon my soul?   50

	Yet I must disappoint thee—I've a place	
	Near school, in Westwood, where I'll plague thee not.	
CHER	Belike thou wouldst prefer a distant school,	
	Upon the eastern coast. They say the lasses	
	Of New York University are plain	55
	And have few standards in their choice of men.	
JOSH	Thou shouldst turn jester, funny as thou art.	

            [Cher opens her music box.

	Nay, we'll not listen to such tripe as this;	
	The news reports are better for our minds.	
CHER	Not in my house an hour, yet thou wouldst force	60
	Thy will on me, dispensing thy commands?	
JOSH	Except where thou and all thy friends reside,	
	Contempo Casual, it is consider'd	
	A virtue excellent to know the matters	
	Affecting broader corners of the globe.	65
CHER	My thanks. In virtue, certainly I need	
	Instruction from a teacher such as thou.	
	Remind me what thou know'st of Kenny G,	
	How silhouettes and songbirds move thy soul?	

Enter MEL HOROWITZ.

	Come, children, join me at the dining table,	70
MEL	Your bickering, which I did overhear,	
	Hath given me a hefty appetite.	

            [They all sit down together.

	Josh, welcome once again unto our home.	
	Art thou yet growing? Thou dost taller seem	
	Than when I last saw thee, at Eastertide.	75
JOSH	Though I have not, of late, ta'en mine own measure,	

	Methinks I am as large as ever was.
MEL	Looks he not bigger unto thine eyes, Cher?
CHER	'Tis possible his head hath grown a size,
	Therein to fit his rising self-esteem. 80
MEL	Hast thou, Josh, given thought to our past talks
	Of corp'rate law and all its benefits?
JOSH	Yea, many greenbacks may be made therewith,
	Yet I would give some green back to the earth
	And mayhap ply environmental law. 85
MEL	Thou wouldst enjoy a sad, frustrating life?
CHER	No matter what Josh does, such shall be his.
MEL	At least the lad knows what he would pursue,
	Whilst thou pursuest only fashion's paths.
	He also doth attend a college fine, 90
	Whilst 'tis not in thy plans.
CHER	—Indeed, I have
	Not gone to Smith.
JOSH	—Go there? Canst even spell it?
MEL	I would see thee have more direction, Cher.
CHER	Nay, Father, for I have direction plenty.
JOSH	Thy compass pointeth mallward, verily. 95
MEL	Our conversation bringeth to my mind
	Today's report card. Shalt thou soon amaze
	As I admire, appreciate thine As?
CHER	Anon, but 'tis not yet prepar'd for thee.
MEL	What meanest thou? Reports were due today, 100
	We had assurance from the school thereof.
CHER	Some teachers, Father, ply egregious schemes
	Upon the tender feelings of thy kin—
	In short, they lowball me most viciously.
	Thy keen advice I, in this matter, heed: 105

"Accept thou ne'er the offer which comes first,
For as is true of wines, antiques, and cheeses,
The thing that ages more may better prove."
The grades receiv'd today are infants mere,
A point from which to ripen, grow, mature—   110
The starting block from which I'll win the race,
The jumping-off point whence I'll higher rise.
Negotiations now begin in earnest.

MEL   In sooth, thou hast well heeded thine old man.

                    Enter MESSENGER.
               All rise as if to answer a summons.

CHER   Is't Dee who calls?
JOSH   —Some message mine?
                              [The messenger hands a note to Mel.
MEL   —For me?   115
              A message come from Jacob. What is it?
                                   [Mel reads the message.
              Nay, nay, my schedule is already full!
                              [Exeunt Mel with the messenger.
CHER   Thou hast the color brown upon thy nose,
              Which marketh how thou begg'st for Father's favor.
JOSH   Thou hast the color black upon thy heart,   120
              A churlish, superficial space cadet.
              How canst thou think thy teachers e'er will change
              The careful and consider'd grades they gave?
CHER   'Tis simple: each semester have I done,
              For teachers are like clay within my hands,   125
              And I a master potter at the wheel.
JOSH   I'll wager thou shalt throw but heaps of mud.

CHER   We shall see who is wrong or right. Adieu.

                                                    [Exit Cher.

JOSH   Ah, though she be but little, she is fierce,
            And hath a pleasing moxie, though I think   130
            Her hollow as a log, so empty that
            A skulk of foxes may reside therein.
            Why doth she wend her way inside my soul,
            To nettle and exasperate me so?
            She is a silly girl, and nothing more—   135
            Why do her insults, then, infect my mind
            As if they were the words of holy writ?
            Forget the matter, Josh, and move thou on.
            Though we awhile may see each other more,
            Unto thy heart to her ope not the door.   140

                                                    [Exit.

SCENE 3

Westside Pavilion mall.

Enter CHER, *holding bags.*

CHER   Most teachers took the bait as I had hop'd—
            In education physical, I told
            My tutor that a spiteful, brutal man
            Had rent my heart in twain deceitfully,
            Told her how I could neither eat nor sleep,   5
            So painful was the matter twixt we two.

She comprehended, totally agreed,
For she was ne'er enamor'd of their sex.
She gladly rais'd my C unto a B—
Concerning unto Better in a trice.   10
I promis'd Lady Geist that I would start
A movement, a campaign of letters sent
Unto the halls of Congress to object
To violations of the Clean Air Act.
One stone, though, even I—a mighty force—   15
Still found immovable and could not budge;
Firm Master Hall was rigid as a rock,
And thrice as hard. He labell'd my debates
Unresearch'd, unconvincing, and unstructur'd—
As if! As if no research I had done,   20
As if mine arguments did not persuade,
As if my points flow'd not sequentially,
As if I were no expert of debate!
I felt most impotent and sans control,
Which is a hateful, irritating state.   25
Some sanctuary needed I, wherein
To gather all my thoughts in one accord,
Regain my strength, that I might be prepar'd
To charge, renew'd, once more unto the breach.
'Tis wherefore I have come unto this place,   30
This refuge mine: Westside Pavilion mall.

Enter DIONNE.

DIONNE   What is the matter on thy heart, sweet friend?
             Thy visage darkens like a dusky eve.
             Dost suffer the remorse of buyers' minds?
CHER   Nay, nothing purchas'd yet hath turn'd regret.   35
             All day within these markets have I roam'd,
             Procuring garments new and sundry trifles,
             Yet inspiration's thunderbolt strikes not.
             No lightning comes, illumining the case
             Of Master Hall and how to change his mind.   40
             Much I've attempted to convince him of
             Mine excellent scholastic aptitude,

	Yet I was brutally rebuff'd each time.	
DIONNE	Be done with all thy Herculean efforts—	
	He is a little, miserable man	45
	Who would make all as desolate as he.	
CHER	Thou hast it, Dee! A true advisor, thou!	
	We must make him exceedingly content.	

Think thou of all we know of Master Hall:
The man is single, sans a paramour,   50
His age is forty-seven, not a youth,
He earneth minor ducats at a job
Wherein he garners little gratitude.
He needeth boinkage in his boring bed.
Unfortunately, his romantic options   55
Are few and far between within our school,
A drought of eligible bach'lorettes,
A female famine for his feasting fire.
The evil, trollish women who teach math
Have husbands, which is most incalculable.   60
The grand tradition of sport teachers lives,
As Lady Stoeger plays but women's games.
Yet what of Lady Geist? I'll not discount
Th'inherent possibilities therein.
Yea, she is oft beset by running stockings,   65
A slip that e'er peeks out beneath her skirt,
More paint upon her teeth than on her lips—
She nearly screams for renovation full.
We two may be the woman's only hope!
Upon the instant, we'll enact our plan: 70
To bring good Lady Geist and Master Hall
Into a mountain of affection, th'one
With th'other. I would fain have it a match,

And I doubt not but soon to fashion it.
[She picks up a quill and paper.
I'll write a letter, signèd only by   75
One who doth call himself Admirer Secret.
[*Writing:*] "Rough winds do shake the darling buds of
                                                            May,
But thy eternal summer shall not fade."

DIONNE   Didst thou create those words, thou clever bard?

CHER   Nay, 'tis a quote from poet much renown'd,   80
          Whom all do read and love—or someday will.

DIONNE   Who is the writer, for I know them not?

CHER   One Clifton Hillegass, of CliffsNotes fame.
          We'll place the letter in her postal box,
          And set her in the path of Master Hall.   85
          If we can do this, Cupid is no longer
          An archer—yea, his glory shall be ours,
          For we're the only love gods, verily.
          Come, let us put the plan to action now,
          And tie the cords of love round them somehow.   90
                                                [Exeunt.

SCENE 4

Bronson Alcott High School.

Enter LADY TOBY GEIST.

GEIST   When love unbidden comes, who can but heed?

This morn, whilst unsuspecting I did go
About the business of a normal day,
Stopp'd I within the office of the school
To check my mailbox, which is normally   5
A task quotidian that merely bores—
Some papers, memoranda, and that sort
Of necessary academic matters.
What mighty change came o'er the mail today!
'Twas like a sorcerer had touch'd the box,   10
Transforming it to a romantic thing.
First did I notice the red rose within,
As colorful as blood that quickens when
A lover whispers in another's ear.
The scent—how fragrant, as if someone had   15
Caught loveliness itself within a smell.
The situation, though, grew finer yet—
The rose became the secondary thrill
When I espied the note that 'neath it sat.
In simple letters, penn'd by tender hand,   20
There was a verse of passing beauty writ,
With signature of one Admirer Secret.
Admirer? Of myself? How can it be?
Ne'er did I think to be the center of
A romance, intrigue, passion such as this.   25
Who at the school—for surely it must be
A member of the staff who sent the note—
Hath eyes for one so humble as myself,
Whose homely face and horrible complexion
Hath caus'd all fervent hope to disappear   30
Of ever winning any man's affection?
The smile that blossom'd on my startled face

Hath only widen'd since this morning's gift.
Admirer Secret, answer shall I give,
For by thine ardor, I know thou art true.   35
I must discover who thou art, sweet friend,
That our two hearts may be combin'd as one!

           [Exit.

       Enter CHER *and* DIONNE.

DIONNE   Didst see the look upon the lady's face
            When she did ope the letter thou didst send?
            How happy look'd she, more than e'er I saw.   40
CHER   A classic tale of romance halfway told—
            We must yet seize upon the other half.

          [They walk into Master Hall's classroom.

Enter MASTER WENDELL HALL. *Enter* MURRAY, TRAVIS,
ELTON, *and other* STUDENTS, *taking their seats.*

HALL   Now Paroudasm Banofshon, thou hast
              Full sixteen tardies thou must work to clear.
PAROUD.   *Sag-e anntar goosaley-e goh*—ha!   45
HALL   Good Janet Hong, no tardies on thy record.
                                          [*Janet smiles.*
              But Travis Birkenstock hath thirty-eight,
              By far the most, as if thou sought the record!
              Congratulations.
                                          [*All applaud.*
TRAVIS   —Unexpected!
              No speech prepar'd I for this honor.   50
              These few words, though, I'd gladly utter:
              The tardy life's the work of many—
              My tardiness by many people
              Created was. Yea, I am grateful
              Unto my parents, ne'er rides giving,   55
              The drivers of the L. A. buses
              Who took a chance upon an unknown.
              Last—not the least—the wonderful crew
              At old McDonalds Inn, that spendeth
              Their hours at cooking Egg McMuffins,   60
              Sans which I never might be tardy.
HALL   Would that thy discourse ever wert so clear.
              An thou no messages political
              Hast to impart, I shall proceed anon.
              Cher Horowitz, two tardies.
CHER   —I object!   65
              Recallest thou the dates of these alleg'd

	And heinous tardies thou accus'st me of?	
HALL	One fell upon last Monday.	
CHER	—Master Hall,	
	I was a rider of the crimson tide,	
	Awash within the surf of burgundy,	70
	My pelvic boat most verily maroon'd.	
	Unto the bathroom I did swiftly fly	
	To capsize not into the vast red sea.	
HALL	Thou speakest of thy women's troubles, so	
	The tardy I shall graciously forgive.	75
CHER	My gratitude. [*Aside:*] And now to hook the fish.	
	[*To Hall:*] Fair Lady Geist spake truly of thy kindness.	
HALL	What meanest thou?	
CHER	—She said, to me alone,	
	That thou art th'only person at the school	
	Who hath a tittle of intelligence.	80

               [*The bell rings. All exeunt except Master Hall.*

HALL	My Lady Geist—indeed, can this be true?	
	Stand I condemn'd by crabbiness so much?	
	All pettiness and petulance, adieu!	
	No glory lives behind the back of such.	
	And, Lady Geist, love on; I will requite thee,	85
	Moving mine old heart to thy loving hand:	
	If thou dost love, mine int'rest shall incite thee	
	To bind our loves up in a holy band;	
	For others say thou dost deserve, and I	
	Shall with thy wooing, loving heart comply.	90

                                          [*Exit.*

SCENE 5

The Horowitz house and
Bronson Alcott High School.

Enter CHER *and* MEL HOROWITZ.

MEL   A word with thee, my daughter.

CHER   —Father, what?

MEL   A message was deliver'd unto me,
             Of which I'd gladly hear thine explanation.
                              [He hands her a paper.

CHER   [*reading:*] "A second notice of outstanding tickets."
             Ne'er was first notice given me, in sooth.   5

MEL   The tickets thou receiv'dst were thy first notice.
             How didst thou, sans a license, tickets earn?

CHER   'Tis simple; tickets come most easily,
             Most anytime they haply wander by.

MEL   Not in my household, nay. From this time hence,   10
             Thou shalt no cart nor carriage operate,
             Nor sit therein sans supervision of
             A licens'd driver watching over thee,
             Which meaneth cruising not with Dionne, either.
             Two permits equal not one license whole—   15
             'Tis neither mathematics nor the law.
             Are my words clear enow?

CHER   —Yea, father kind.

MEL   It is the fondest hope of me, thy father,
             That thou becom'st a driver safe and good.
             When thou dost put thy mind unto the task,   20

	Thou mayst accomplish nearly anything.
CHER	I shall, and with new purpose soon will practice.
MEL	'Tis well. And now to work. Adieu, dear heart.

[Exit Mel.

CHER   A licens'd driver who hath naught to do—
Where shall I find a loser such as this,   25
A unicorn of such partic'lar skill?
Ah, Josh approacheth, as if summon'd by
Mine urgent need, his horn already prim'd.

Enter JOSH, *reading.*

JOSH   [*aside:*] Past good and evil is the will to pow'r,
The dawn of day shall see the antichrist—   30
At least, so writes this grim philosopher.

CHER   What is upon thy chin, granola breath?
Some dirt? Perchance a speck of errant dust?
Or is it manly hair that I espy?

JOSH   A fash'nable goatee thereon doth grow.   35

CHER   'Tis well, for then thou shalt not be the last
Who, in the coffeehouse, some chin pubes hath.

JOSH   Words fail t'express how much my heart doth leap
When we have conversations such as this,
For always 'tis a joy to speak with thee.   40
'Tis clear, however, that thou something want'st,
So wherefore not save us both energy
And time, and tell me what thou wilt anon.

CHER   Indeed. My driver's permit I possess,
With which I am allow'd to drive, yet Father   45
Saith he'd not have me take the carriage out
Sans someone licens'd who would go withal.

            Thou hast no matters of importance—

JOSH   —Ha!

            What chance have I that thou shalt shut thy mouth

            Ere thou convincest me to do thy bidding?   50

CHER   In sooth, 'tis slim to none. Let us away!

JOSH   [*aside:*] I'll go, for I am human, all too human.

                      [They climb into the carriage.

                      Cher drives as Josh observes.

            [*To Cher:*] Thou drivest like James Bond, the British spy,

            And I've no time to die today, in sooth!

            Yet in America we drive upon   55

            The right side of the road, Cher, not the left.

CHER   An thou didst hold the reins in platform shoes,

            'Twould not be easy for thee either, Josh.

JOSH   Soon I must make return unto my school.

            Wouldst practice parking, ere our time is through?   60

CHER   What need have I to park, when nearly each

            Establishment hath valets for the task?

JOSH   [*aside:*] By heav'n, the lass is spoil'd like worm-fill'd

                                  fruit.

CHER   What class is thine today?

JOSH   —If thou wouldst know,

            I have a meeting with TreePeople now—   65

            'Tis possible Sir Mark E. Mark shall come

            To plant a tree and, by the action, shall

            Share his celebrity with our good cause.

CHER   How fabulous, Sir Mark E. Mark indeed!

            A wonder 'tis he hath the time for ye—   70

            Amidst his active, busy calendar

            Of dropping pantaloons—to plant a tree.

            Why would your group not hire a gardener?

JOSH   Perchance Sir Mark E. Mark doth wish to use
            His popularity for acts of good   75
            And make a contribution to the world?
            In case the word is foreign to thine ears,
            A contribution is—

CHER   —Excuse me, imp,
            Full many fine Italian outfits have
            I giv'n to Lucy, and when I procure   80
            My license, I shall brake for animals.
            Additionally, I have spent my time
            In helping lonely souls—two teachers mine—
            Find romance in their sad and empty lives.

JOSH   Belike such serves thine in'trests more than theirs.   85
            If e'er an action of the noble Cher
            Were not nine parts of ten her benefit,
            'Tis possible I'd die of instant shock.

CHER   Such would be impetus enow for me.
                            [They arrive at Cher's school.
                            Cher climbs out of the carriage.

JOSH   Our lesson endeth for the present time.   90
            Mine impetus is to leave is strong, since thou
            Hast call'd me imp and wish'd mine early death.
            Farewell. Enjoy thy perfect, pleasant life.
                            [Exit Josh in carriage.

CHER   His words like slivers sink beneath my skin
            And fester. Is my reputation thus?   95
            Am I so shallow and so callous, too,
            That he imagines me so self-absorb'd?

                        Enter DIONNE.

	O, Dionne, tell me true: wouldst call me selfish?
DIONNE	Not to thy face.
CHER	—Indeed?
DIONNE	—Why art thou sad?

I saw thee when thou didst arrive with Josh.   100
Hath he fill'd up thy mind with muck and filth,
Born from his present notions, meaning his
Postadolescent idealistic phase?

CHER   Behold, 'tis Master Hall. The game's afoot!

Enter MASTER WENDELL HALL.

DIONNE	Ho, Master Hall!
CHER	—We bid thee, walk with us. 105

Dost thou drink coffee, nectar of the gods?

HALL   Not from our cafeteria—their grounds
Do earn the name, in tasting just like dirt.
Yet under normal circumstances, yea.

CHER   I am a fool! Today, as I did pack   110
My lunch, I accident'lly switch'd my drink
With my sweet father's—he hath lemonade
Whilst I am saddl'd with his bitter flask—
Italian roasted coffee, which I loathe.
Wouldst thou the pleasure of the auburn drink?   115

HALL   Thou dost desire it not?

CHER   —'Twould stunt my growth.
I hope to grow to inches three score ten,
Like mine exemplar, Lady Cindy Crawford.
Methought thou mightest like to share the drink
With Lady Geist—or someone else. Or her.   120

HALL   [*aside:*] A brilliant notion! [*To them:*] Girls, my
                                                    gratitude.

       CHER *hands him the coffee.* MASTER HALL
         walks aside. Enter LADY TOBY GEIST.

CHER   Kind Lady Geist! Thy timing is profound.
GEIST   Good morning, girls. Have ye secur'd your places
            In our environmental fete that comes?
DIONNE   We shall anon.
CHER   —Thine eyes, how beautiful.   125
            Hide them not underneath these spectacles.
                         [*Cher removes Lady Geist's glasses.*
DIONNE   Thy doublet should be tied around thy waist,
            Which is as small as any lass could dream.
                         [*Dionne ties Lady Geist's doublet
                              around the lady's waist.*
CHER   These clips restrain thy hair's cascading locks,
            Which should be free to fall about thy shoulders.   130
                         [*Cher removes the clips from Lady Geist's hair.*
GEIST   Such fond and strange attention ye do show.
            Forget ye not th'environmental fair!
                              [*Lady Geist walks aside.*
DIONNE   She is no perfect beauty, by my troth,
            Yet the improvement is immediate.
CHER   We did construct the strongest edifice   135
            With those few, meager tools that were at hand.
            Come, friend—let us with haste proceed unto
            Our class of education physical.
                         [*The girls begin walking toward their next class.*
DIONNE   I would not go today, it tires my soul.

CHER   Full well I know th'exhaustion of thy heart.   140
              Still, though, I'll warrant sport shall do us good—
              Of late my body feels most heiferlike,
              All weight and hips and udders ev'rywhere,
              Like I had stomachs four that I must fill.
              Today I had two bowls of Special K,   145
              Three pieces of delightful turkey bacon,
              A full hand's worth of popp'd corn most delicious,
              Five peanut butter M and Ms—

DIONNE   —Behold!
              [Master Hall approaches Lady Geist and they
                   sit together, sharing the container of coffee.
              A scene that doth befit a portrait grand,
              Created by the master artists—us!   150

CHER   Behold the language of their bodies two,
              Which one may read as if 'twere English words—
              Their legs both cross'd toward the other one,
              An invitation unequivocal
              Unto an intimate encounter. O!   155
              Read thereupon the triumph of our match.

DIONNE   See how she giveth him her address, that
              He soon may call upon her where she lives.
              The digits she gives up most willingly.
              Behold our Lady Geist, so cute and touch'd.   160

CHER   Who knew the elderly could be so sweet?
              Let us to class, upon contented feet.
                        [Exeunt Cher and Dionne. Master Hall and
                             Lady Geist say farewells. Exit Lady Geist.

HALL   Astounding days, when liking turns to love,
              When colleagues two become a pair entwin'd.
              'Tis early days, and yet 'tis like I've known   165

The lady all my life, was meant by fate
To dwell within her presence evermore.
No more shall I neglect my outward look,
But groom myself to mate and court and woo.
If I can win her, great shall be the heist—   170
This Wendell Hall shall capture Toby Geist!

           [Exit.

ACT II

SCENE 1

The Horowitz house.

Enter BALTHASAR *on balcony.*

BALTHASAR　[*singing:*] The world is fill'd with fools
　　　　　　　Who never act aright,
　　　　　They know what they do
　　　　　　　As daytime turns to night.
　　　　　So pretty thou, so silly thou,　　　　　　5
　　　　　　　So wondrously alive,
　　　　　O, change thou ne'er, be mine fore'er,
　　　　　　　Put down thy foot and drive.
　　　　　Thou, be not like those fools,
　　　　　　　Pray, come with me, we'll fly—　　　10
　　　　　Thou nothing hast to lose,
　　　　　　　If thou shalt only try.
　　　　　So pretty thou, so silly thou,
　　　　　　　So wondrously alive,
　　　　　O, change thou ne'er, &c.　　　　　　　15
　　　　　Thou art so pretty, dear,
　　　　　　　Yet never satisfied—
　　　　　Search, then, for something new,
　　　　　　　For thou hast naught to hide.
　　　　　So pretty thou, so silly thou,　　　　　20
　　　　　　　So wondrously alive,
　　　　　O, change thou ne'er, &c.

　　　　　　　　　　　　　　　[Exit Balthasar.

Enter CHER.

CHER   The grades that Master Hall dispenseth hath
            Arisen—yea, not only just for me,
            But for the class entire. I've earn'd their praise,   25
            For all do know 'twas Dionne and myself
            Who put our Master Hall in better spirits
            Through his relationship with Lady Geist.
            When our last papers were return'd to us,
            How great was the rejoicing of the class.   30
            Young Elton did embrace me ardently
            To show his thanks. Meanwhile, we did espy
            The couple, Lady Geist and Master Hall,
            Engag'd in kisses deep ere they departed.
            The plan hath work'd e'en better than we hop'd!   35
            Last Friday, Lady Geist wrote on the board
            Our homework for the weekend soon to come,
            Yet wrote she merely, "Have ye fun!" and smil'd,
            As if she plann'd to heed her own advice—
            Yea, assignation shall be her assignment.   40

Enter MEL HOROWITZ.

MEL   Cher, canst thou proffer any explanation?
CHER   Thou speakest of my new report card, sir?
MEL   The same semester 'tis? Have I this right?
CHER   Indeed.
MEL   —What magic dark hast thou perform'd?
            Thy grade for education physical   45
            Hath turn'd into an A, such I expected—
            A simple subject, simple was the change.

Yet how hast thou these other subjects alter'd?
Debate: thy C transform'd into an A.
World history: a B turn'd A as well.   50
What spell hast thou cast over these two teachers,
This Master Hall and Lady Geist, that they
Were willing to enhance thy marks so much?
Some extra credit and reports to match?

CHER   Nay, Father.

MEL   —Didst thou, then, retake thy tests?   55

CHER   Nay, neither this.

MEL   —Thou wouldst have me believe
Thou—by thine arguments—hath climbèd so,
Ascended from a C unto an A?

CHER   Completely by my powers of persuasion.
Is thy heart bursting with o'erwhelming pride?   60

MEL   Forsooth, no prouder could I be, e'en if
Those grades were based on merit. O, well done!

                                    [*They embrace.*

My clever daughter, apple of mine eye,
Inheritor of all thy mother's wit,
And pure delight unto thy father, too.   65
Tonight, we'll celebrate this feat of thine.

                                    [*Exit Cher.*

To raise a daughter by myself was ne'er
What I had hop'd before her mother died.
How could I cope with such a loss as hers,
How could I hope to serve as parent double?   70
Amidst my grief, which foreign was to me,
I vow'd to raise my Cher as best I could.
'Twas years ago, yet feels like yesterday.
As one doth parent, 'tis impossible

To know if, day to day, one does aright.   75
As if I were the pilot of a boat
Who sail'd, sans compass or a map, across
The ocean vast, I could not see the goal,
But merely hop'd to steer in the direction
That soon would set us safe upon the shore.   80
To hear of Cher's astute and cunning ways
Tells me she hath a depth I realiz'd not,
An anchor deep that keeps her firmly rooted.
My wondrous daughter, now 'tis plain to me—
Together we shall cross th'expansive sea.   85

[Exit.

SCENE 2

Bronson Alcott High School and the Horowitz house.

Enter CHER *in tennis clothes.*

CHER   So satisfying was my father's joy
That I am mov'd to render more good deeds
Upon the other people hereabout.

Enter DIONNE, AMBER, LADY STOEGER, *and
various* STUDENTS *in tennis clothes.*

DIONNE   Ah-choo!
CHER   —Dee, when thine allergies arise,

| | Take out the ring within thy pretty nose, | 5 |

Take out the ring within thy pretty nose, 5
That it not in thy mucous be engulf'd.

STOEGER   Cher, 'tis thy turn to hit the balls with me.

[Cher continues talking to Dee.

Attend! Respond thou to my calling voice!

CHER   Apologies, good Lady Stoeger, that
I did not heed thee when thou first did call. 10
One word, too: education physical
Within our school is reprehensible—
To stand in line for forty minutes whilst
We wait to take a turn and swat a ball
Is not aerobic'lly effective, nay. 15
In such a fruitless period of time,
I could not shed the calories found in
A paltry stick of Carefree gum.

STUDENTS   [*applauding:*]   —Hurrah!

STOEGER   If not thy body, certainly thy mouth
Hath had excessive exercise, in faith. 20
Hit thou the balls that cometh unto thee.

CHER   When I have match'd my racket to these balls,
I shall, indeed, by heaven, play a set.
These balls, though, which do whir past me so fast,
Belike shall strike my crown into the hazard. 25
The sleek machine that shoots them like a cannon
Is full of danger, Lady Stoeger, with
A massive lawsuit waiting in the wings.

STOEGER   My gratitude for this, thy legal counsel.
Come, Dionne, 'tis thy turn.

DIONNE   —Yet Lady Stoeger, 30
I bear a note from mine own tennis coach.
He would prefer if I did not expose

             Myself to any training that, perchance,
             May overturn his better principles.

STOEGER   [*aside:*] Pray, give me patience. [*To Dionne:*] Thou,
                               then, art excus'd.   35
             Come, Amber, to the fray.

AMBER   —Nay, Lady Stoeger,
             My plastic surgeon would have me avoid
             Activities wherein there may be balls
             That fly in the direction of my nose.

DIONNE   Alas for thee, thy social life is o'er.   40

       Enter TAI *accompanied by a* TEACHER.

TEACHER   Good Lady Stoeger, here's another one—
             A student new to join the merry ranks.
             Take heed, I prithee, ladies: bid ye welcome
             Unto your newfound friend, Tai Frasier she.
                              [Exit teacher.

STOEGER   Thou hast no time to change thy clothing, Tai,   45
             Yet may still strike at balls in what thou wear'st.

AMBER   In what she weareth, she could farmer be!

CHER   [*aside, to Dionne:*] Dee, mine assignment now is clear
                                 to me:
             Behold the girl, adorably clueless.
             We shall adopt her, make her one of us.   50

DIONNE   The woman is toe up. Our stock shall fall
             Should we expend our time with such as she.

CHER   Dee, think of it: dost thou not wish to use
             Thy popularity in acts of good,
             A contribution making to the world?   55

DIONNE   Nay, such beneficence ne'er cross'd my mind.

CHER   [to Tai:] Come hither! We would speak with thee awhile.
                              [Tai approaches Cher and Dionne.

TAI   My thanks, 'tis passing lonesome to be new.

CHER   Art thou enjoying California, Tai?

TAI   In troth, my mind runs wild without surcease.   60
              Hast thou some herbal remedy for me?

DIONNE   The time for lunch arrives ten minutes hence.
              We have no tea, yet do have Coke for thee.

TAI   Ye coke do have, the leaves of coca trees?

                    The bell rings. Enter more STUDENTS,
                    including MURRAY, TRAVIS, and ELTON.

CHER   This is America—we've Coke for all.   65
              Let us show thee the ins and outs and wheres
              Of Bronson Alcott High School. Let us fly!
                    [Cher, Dionne, and Tai walk around the school
                    grounds, looking at various groups of students.
              Behold Alana's group, the players they,
              Who are of their own stage too well enamor'd.
              The Persian mafia are gather'd yon,   70
              Whom none can join without a carriage fine—
              A Bayerische Motoren Werke.
              There is one Elton, in the vest of white,
              'Midst the most popular in all the school.

DIONNE   Including Murray, mine own paramour.   75
              Is he not handsome?

TAI   —Yea, he is indeed!

CHER   Shouldst thou debase thyself and date a lad
              Who still in high school is, 'tis from that group
              Thou must select; acceptable are they.

TAI   Which one of them is thine, then, Cher?

CHER   —As if!   80
             As if I would date one in high school still,
             As if I find them not too immature,
             As if my place were not above them all,
             As if they are not monkeys, verily!

DIONNE   Cher hath too much of pride and prejudice   85
             When turns the subject unto high school lads.

CHER   'Tis but a choice—important, personal—
             Which ev'ry woman must make for herself.

                                [Murray approaches them.

MURRAY   My lass, lend me five ducats presently.

DIONNE   Again and still again have I bid thee   90
             Not summon me with such a word as lass.
             'Tis too informal—disrespectful, too.
             Call me not lass, lad—Dionne is my name.

MURRAY   Beg pardon, Madame Dionne, if thou wilt.

DIONNE   My thanks.

MURRAY   —Consider thou this point: street slang,   95
             The idioms and language coming thence,
             Increasingly is valid as a form
             T'express oneself. Its pronouns feminine,
             I shall admit, indeed have somewhat mocking—
             Yet not misogynistic—undertones.   100

                                *[Murray and Dionne smile at
                                 each other. Exit Murray.*

TAI   The words come forth from ye like older folk,
             Not childish like those to whom I'm accustom'd.

CHER   This school is excellent in ev'ry way,
             A credit to the man whose name it bears:
             One Amos Bronson Alcott, father to   105

Some gifted little women long ago.

TAI   I do desire a soda, to refresh
My palate. May I get ye one as well?

CHER   'Twould be delightful. Many thanks, sweet Tai.
                              [Tai walks aside, toward the cafeteria.

DIONNE   The lady is delightful—thou wert right.   110

CHER   A project for us both! I'll warrant, Dee,
The time shall not go dully by us.

DIONNE   —Heigh!
                              *[Dionne and Cher sit just outside the
                              cafeteria. Tai waits in line next to Travis.*

TRAVIS   *[to Tai:]* O wow, this food is most disgusting.
                                        [Tai laughs.

I see the drawing on thy notebook—
'Tis a representation wondrous.   115

TAI   How kind thy words! The emblems on thy board—
Four-wheel'd, for skating quickly 'cross the grounds—
Are well array'd.
                              [They look at Travis's skateboard.

TRAVIS   —O, think'st thou so, yea?
Methought they were mayhap too clutter'd.
My plan is soon to wipe the slate clear   120
To focus on a decorative
Main statement in the center of it,
Like Marvin—he, the Martian—thereon.

TAI   Coincidence beyond the pow'rs of heav'n!
I many times have drawn this Marvin, too,   125
And could for thee arrange an illustration.

TRAVIS   Indeed? Ability so wondrous!

TAI   Nay, there is little to the character,
A simple series of both lines and circles.

	Wouldst see the sketches in my book?
TRAVIS	—Yea!
TAI	Behold.

[She shows him drawings in her notebook.

TRAVIS	—A spectacle amazing!
TAI	My thanks.
TRAVIS	—Thou drewest that by thy hand?
TAI	Forsooth, and more on pages subsequent.
TRAVIS	Thou didst not trace these from some other?
TAI	Nay, 'twas the work of mine own hand, I swear.
	Behold another—oft have I drawn him.
TRAVIS	Is not that lovely? [*Aside:*] She is also!
TAI	Thou canst see other characters as well,
	Such merry doodles of my wand'ring hand.
TRAVIS	They are as cute as ever I saw!
TAI	To draw is my delight.
TRAVIS	—Thou skill'd art!
TAI	Nay, 'tis a trifle.
TRAVIS	—I'm in earnest—
	Thy talent no comparison hath.

[Tai joins Cher and Dionne, who eat
their lunches. Travis sits elsewhere.

DIONNE	[*to Cher:*] The food thou eatest, is it truly free
	Of ev'ry element that causeth fat?
CHER	Yea, and one loseth weight by cutting it
	Into far smaller bites than usual.
	'Tis science, pure and simple.
TAI	—Ladies, heed:
	I've met a man who caus'd my heart to swoon.
CHER	Describe him to us, we may know the lad.
TAI	His hair is long, cascades like waterfall,

130

135

140

145

150

His wit is humorous beyond compare,
Match'd only by his generosity,
For quickly did he proffer me some smoke—
Behold him there!

> *[She waves to Travis, who waves*
> *back, dropping his food.*

CHER   —By smoke, thou meanest drugs?   155

TAI   Yea, for to aid my creativity
I keep invention in a noted weed.

CHER   Tai, tell me plainly: what is thy young age?

TAI   Sixteen in May.

CHER   —My birthday is in April.
As someone older, wiser than thyself,   160
I must, perforce, share with thee some advice.
'Tis one thing to partake of doobies at
A party, where one sparketh up with friends;
Yet 'tis another quite to be fried always,
Thy brain e'er poison'd. I do know his spirit,   165
And will not trust one lazy as he with
A drug of such damn'd nature. Those he has
Will stupefy and dull the sense awhile;
With which, perchance, he first shall bake himself.

DIONNE   Canst thou see the distinction twixt these two: 170
A social smoking versus constant flames?

TAI   Methinks I can.

CHER   —Their type, the loadies, hang
About the grassy knoll, with hacky sacks.
They come to class and say their foolish lines—
Which we, as at a jester, laugh withal—   175
Yet no lass of respectable renown
Would seek a paramour among their kind.

	Thou wouldst not start thy journey with a step	
	Ta'en in the wrong direction, wouldst thou?	
TAI	—Nay.	
CHER	A notion comes to mind that thou mayst like—	180
	Shall we give thee a makeover, my friend?	
DIONNE	'Twould be a joy!	
TAI	—Nay, 'tis not fit for me.	
DIONNE	Let us, I pray. 'Tis Cher's main joy in life	
	To play at making over her companions.	
	It giveth her a sense of full control	185
	Amidst of world of chaos and confusion—	
	'Midst such a calm her talents flourish quite.	
CHER	I prithee, let us!	
TAI	—Wherefore not? We shall!	
	Unusual this is, my friends, that I	
	Should have compeers responsible as ye.	190
CHER	Thy meaning, Tai, is enigmatical,	
	Yet let us homeward after school today	
	Where we this matter shall with joy pursue!	
	The reddish dye we'll lather from your hair,	
	And paint thy face to seem most natural,	195
	Whilst curling thine already wavy locks.	
	Thy clothes we shall with scissors shorten, that	
	Thy shirts expose some of thy lovely waist.	
	My closet, too, shall open'd be for thee,	
	That we may choose new garments thou mayst wear.	200

[Exeunt all students except Cher,
Dionne, and Tai, who go to Cher's
house and change Tai's appearance.

Enter BALTHASAR *on balcony.*

BALTHASAR   [*singing:*] I care not what my teachers say,
                     A supermodel I shall be!
                 Yea, ev'ryone shall dress my way,
                     Wait for a trice and you shall see!
                 When supermodel I become,   205
                     My hair shall shine an 'twere the sea!
                 From shore to shore the people come
                     To learn how they may look like me!
                             [Exit Balthasar. Cher and Dionne
                             look at Tai, who is transformed.

CHER   Aerobic exercise is just the thing
                 To keep thy body supple, lean, and fit.   210

DIONNE   I shall away, that you may have your sport.
                         [Exit Dionne. Cher and Tai exercise.

TAI   Alas, I am too tir'd to carry on.
                 Mine aching buns, they lack the feel of steel.

CHER   Each day's exertions shall grow easier,
                 If thou be active ev'ry passing day,   215
                 And not sporadic'lly as thou mayst wish.

TAI   How does one know if 'tis sporadic'lly?
                 Methinks I may hurt my sporadic nerve.

                 Enter JOSH, *unseen and listening.*

CHER   "Sporadic nerve"? Alas, it seemeth thy
                 Vocabulary is sporadic, too.   220
                 We must work with thy words and accent, if
                 Thou wouldst be as presentable as I.
                 Mayhap thou shouldst repeat this phrase hereafter:
                 "The rain in Spain stays mainly in the plain."
                 Learn, too, the meaning of this useful word: 225

    Sporadic means once in a while, my dear.
    Try thou to use it, sometime, in thy speech,
    That thou becom'st accustom'd to its sound.
TAI   I shall, an it make me as wise as thee.
CHER Hereafter, we shall cross-train, switching twixt 230
    Our Lady Cindy Crawford's masterwork—
    Aerobicize, Zounds!—and that classic tome
    Of fitness, even *Steely Buns*. Past this,
    We shall both read one book—not school assign'd—
    For education and enjoyment both.   235
    My first selection's *Fit or Fat—Forsooth!*
TAI   Mine is the timeless interstellar tale:
    Men Hail from Mars, Whilst Women Hail from Venus.
CHER An excellent selection, by my troth.

Thereby—with these exertions and these books—   240
Our minds and bodies both shall be improv'd.
Yet something, still, is lacking in our plan,
A means whereby to help humanity,
And show our ample generosity—
Endeavoring at least one hour or two.   245

JOSH   [*coming forward:*] Good even, wise ones.

CHER   [*aside:*]   —Fie, the
                                                dreaded ex.
         [*To Tai:*] Tai, this is Josh, my ex-stepbrother he.

JOSH   Well met, milady.

CHER   —Thou these matters know'st—
         I would do something for humanity,
         Some good to make my mark upon the world.   250

JOSH   Sterilization is a noble path,
         To share no more Chers with a world in pain.

TAI   Ha, ha! A jest!
                         [*Josh walks aside, to the kitchen,
                                        and Cher follows.*

CHER   —Canst thou be serious?
         What dost thou think of mine ambitious plan?

JOSH   I am amaz'd.

CHER   —That I so humbly give   255
         Myself unto another person's growth
         With generosity and talent both?

JOSH   Nay, that thou someone e'en more clueless than
         Thyself hast found to worship at thy feet.

CHER   Nay, I have rescued her from teenage hell—   260
         Th'unspoken-of tenth level, worst of all,
         Wherein burn jealous snipes and gossip snakes,
         Unending misery for all within,

	For wounds of adolescence never heal—	
	Lasciate ogni speranza, voi ch'entrate!	265
JOSH	Thou, sans a mother of thine own, inflict'st	
	Thy fantasies of motherhood on her	
	Like she were Barbie, thou her *alma mater*.	
CHER	Profound psychology of freshman year	
	Doth rear its head: Annoying 101.	270
JOSH	Nay, I'm no student of psychology.	
CHER	The lost soul thou hast seen with me today	
	Shall soon be well array'd and popular,	
	Two things that thou most certainly are not.	
	Her life shall better be because of me.	275
JOSH	Another thing I certainly am not.	
CHER	How many women could say thus of thee,	
	That they were much improvèd by your presence?	

[They return to Tai.

TAI	[*singing to herself:*] The fresh is better, when 'tis Mentos	
	fresh,	
	So fond and full of life!	280
	[*Speaking:*] The freshmaker, e'en Mentos! What a song.	
JOSH	'Twas my great pleasure making thine acquaintance.	
	I hope our paths shall cross again soon, Tai.	
TAI	Yea, not sporadic'lly.	
JOSH	[*aside:*] —I cannot tell	
	If this is an improvement or decline.	285

[Exit Josh.

| CHER | Come, let us back to school and show thee off— | |
| | I'll wager some shall not believe their eyes. | |

They walk back to school.
Enter DIONNE, *joining them on the way.*

DIONNE   Holla again, friends. Tai, thou comely art—
                Thy new appearance fits thine inward beauty.

                Enter various STUDENTS *as* CHER, TAI, *and*
                     DIONNE *enter the school grounds.*

CHER   Behold how all the lads do baldly gawp,   290
                As if they ne'er had beauty seen before!
                Such an effect upon the weaker sex—
                My heart doth burst for this, my Tai that binds.
DIONNE   Indeed, my soul is kvelling at the sight!

                          Enter TRAVIS.

TRAVIS   Cher, may I ask of thee a question?   295
CHER   Thou hast. Art done?
TRAVIS   —Doth Deamer teach thee?
CHER   Nay, I have Geist.
TRAVIS   —Thou art well met, Tai—
                Didst thou receive a flyer from me?
TAI   Nay, I have none.
TRAVIS   —I prithee, take this.
                          [*He hands her a flyer and exits.*

TAI   Unto a party hath he summon'd me.   300
CHER   'Tis in the Valley. Surely the police
                Shall stop the partying ere it begins—
                Within an hour, which is how long it takes
                To make the voyage thither anyhow.
DIONNE   The guest list shall be local loadies, too.   305
TAI   Yet think ye Travis shall attend as well?
                I would delight to see him once again,

	Especially within a social context.	
DIONNE	Methought thou hadst mov'd on from thoughts of him.	
CHER	I prithee, do not sell thyself so short—	310
	Thou hast some capital none other hath.	
TAI	Nay, nay, my maidenhead is not intact.	
DIONNE	[*aside:*] No virgin she? I scann'd her high and low,	
	And neither hide nor hair of this did grasp.	
CHER	Nay, better yet—thou art a mystery.	315
	As far as all concernèd are, thou art	
	The lass most popular within the school.	
	The fact thou art a friend of Dee and I—	
DIONNE	With humble spirit, I shall speak the truth:	
	It speaketh very highly of thy worth.	320
CHER	If thou dost strike while searing is the iron,	
	Thou shalt select whatever boy thou wish'st.	
TAI	Who dost thou have in mind?	
CHER	—Let me consider	
	The lads who are available. A-ha!	
	The answer cometh quickly. Elton!	
DIONNE	—Yea!	325
CHER	He and Folette broke recently enow.	
TAI	Who is this Elton?	
DIONNE	—One most popular,	
	Like one who doth our social crew direct,	
	To pull us all together as a group.	
CHER	His dad is well-connected 'mongst musicians—	330
	Thou shalt be welcom'd unto any concert.	
	I saw him gazing yesterday on thee,	
	As if he had a pow'rful periscope	
	And thou wert some impressive, looming ship.	
TAI	Look'd he on me?	

CHER   —Yea, and declar'd that thou   335
          Didst make his tooth ache.
TAI   —Nay, how did I so?
CHER   'Tis an expression, telling of thy sweetness.
          So sweet thou art, his tooth did ache thereby.
TAI   Indeed? The lad's kind words could send a mouth
          Entire to staggering in agony.   340

                                        [Exit Tai.

DIONNE   Are thy words true? Spake Elton thus of her?
CHER   Nay. Mayhap, though, he shall when he knows her.
DIONNE   Thou art a naughty lady, I aver!

                                        [Exeunt.

SCENE 3

The Horowitz house.

Enter BALTHASAR *on balcony.*

BALTHASAR   [*singing:*] We are young, we run green,
                    Keep our teeth passing clean,
               See our friends, gaze on sights,
                    Nonny non, feel alright!

                                        [Exit Balthasar.

Enter CHER, *painting a portrait. Enter* DIONNE, TAI,
MURRAY, ELTON, AMBER, *and* SUMMER, *posing for her.*

CHER   O gather ye together, lovely friends.   5
              Pray, Murray, give thy Dionne one small kiss,
              That I may catch the vision on my canvas.
              Smile, all, especially thou, lovely Tai—
              Draw nearer unto Elton. Closer, still.
              Thou, Elton, make thine arm encircle Tai,   10
              To draw her in and make the picture whole.

ELTON   [aside:] So shall I do for thy sake, Cher, not hers.

CHER   A grouping beauteous, my splendid friends.
              Here, Tai, take thou this flower in thy hand,
              Which shall augment thy beauty natural.   15

ELTON   'Tis plain thou art a master artist, Cher.

CHER   Doth Tai not marv'lous look?

ELTON   —She's beautiful.

CHER   A woman with a Botticelli frame,
              Of reddish locks and loveliness profound,
              Who off the canvas leapeth, as if she   20
              Could not within a painting be constrain'd.

ELTON   Whatever portraits thou dost draw of her
              I'd gladly have a copy of, in sooth.

CHER   My pleasure 'tis to furnish thee therewith!
                   [She hands him a portrait of Tai.
              [To all:] My thanks, dear friends, that ye did sit for me. 25
               [Exeunt all but Cher and Tai, who sit together.
              Didst hear the words that pour'd from Elton's mouth?
              He took thy picture! Thinks thee beautiful!
              Mine expectations greatly are surpass'd.

TAI   Miraculous, and I have thee to thank.

Enter MEL HOROWITZ.

CHER	Good even, Father. This is my friend, Tai.	30
MEL	[*to Tai:*] No other greeting can I make but this:	
	Sit not upon my chair. I bid thee, move!	

TAI *moves to another chair. Enter* LUCY, *serving food.*

CHER	I thank thee, Lucy—this doth look delicious.
LUCY	[*aside:*] Her father shall not like it—get me hence!
	[*Exit Lucy in haste.*

MEL	What is this refuse, which I shall refuse?	35
CHER	It cometh from the pages sacrosanct	
	Of *Cut Cholesterol*, a vital tome.	
	Thy Doctor Lovett says thy weight must drop	
	'Til 'tis fourteen and one-half stone or less.	
	[*A bell rings.*	

MEL	No messages tonight.	
CHER	—O, Father, pray:	40
	It's Dionne, and may be important.	
MEL	—Nay!	
	Apologies, yet we shall eat in peace,	
	Like other fam'lies in their happy homes.	
	What happen'd unto thee in school today?	
CHER	Of all the classes I attended and	45
	The lectures that I heard, this mov'd me most:	
	My purple clogs I finally broke in.	

The bell rings again. Enter a MESSENGER *to*
speak to MEL. *Enter* DIONNE *severally.*

DIONNE	[*whispering:*] Cher, Cher!
CHER	[*aside, to Dionne:*] —Dee, what is it?

DIONNE   —I bid thee, hear:
                My Murray studieth geometry
                Near where young Elton's locker may be found.   50
                He spied, within, the portrait thou didst paint
                Of Tai.

CHER   [*aloud:*] —By heaven!

TAI   —What? What is it, Cher?

CHER   Thy picture doth adorn sweet Elton's locker.

TAI   O my!

DIONNE   [*aside, to Cher:*] —The crew entire unto the Valley
                Shall travel to a party presently.   55
                Wilt thou withal?

CHER   [*aside, to Dionne:*] —We shall, to claim Tai's fate!
                Now, get thee gone, my father doth return!
                He doth expect thee not, and, verily,
                The man is in a frightful mood today.

                                        [*Exit Dionne.*

TAI   Surprising turn! O, I am nearly faint!   60

CHER   Bear up, for we must to the Valley soon,
                This party we'll attend—for thee, a boon.

                                        [*Exeunt.*

SCENE 4

The Valley and environs.

Enter DIONNE *and* MURRAY *in his carriage.*

MURRAY   Gaze thou upon the map, toward the top—
            Sun Valley is due north.
DIONNE   —Nay, just Bel Air,
            Where they sip juice out of a champagne glass,
            Though I have heard they're prissy—bourgeois, too.
MURRAY   Thine eyes misguide thee, on the wrong map look.   5
            What is the number writ upon the top?
DIONNE   No numbers there, but letters.
MURRAY   —Fie, enow!

> *They stop. Enter* CHER *and* TAI, *climbing into*
> *the carriage with them. They drive on.*

CHER   Remember, Tai, be sure that Elton sees
            Thee first, but be thou not the first to speak.
            Appear delighted by the company,   10
            The night, with all its splendor and its thrills.
            Look like the lass most popular of all,
            And truly ev'ryone shall think thee thus.
            If thou hast conversation with a lad,
            Talk to his eyeline, look thou never down.   15
            Approach no one, yet let them come to thee.
            Be thou most prudent—give thy thoughts no tongue,
            Nor any unproportion'd thought its act.
            Be thou familiar, but by no means vulgar.
            When thou art speaking with a man, make some   20
            Excuse to leave the dialogue too soon—
            Thus thou shalt ever keep him wanting more.
            Dost understand?
TAI   —I do!
CHER   —Apt pupil, thou!

The carriage stops and all disembark. Enter many STUDENTS
at the party including ELTON, AMBER, SUMMER, *and*
LAWRENCE. *Enter* TRAVIS, *doing a trick on a skateboard.*

TRAVIS   Be ready, for I soar o'er your heads!

                              [Travis rides aside.

TAI   Didst see how he, like bird majestic, flew?   25

CHER   A board on skates shall not impress me, Tai—
         Five years ago 'twas trendy, now 'tis lame.

TRAVIS   [*approaching:*] You came unto the party—brilliant!
           [*To Tai:*] Wouldst like some beer? For I can fetch it.

                      [Travis scampers off to get a drink.

CHER   I prithee, guard thyself from all his charms.   30

              [Cher, Dionne, Tai, and Murray enter the house.

MURRAY   A-ha! A festival of merry souls!

TAI   A wondrous gathering!

CHER   —We'll walk one lap,
         Perambulate round the perimeter
         Ere we commit to any one location.

                      *[A woman begins dancing with
                      Murray. Dionne pushes her aside.*

DIONNE   Who was that wench, and wherefore danc'st with her?   35

MURRAY   Nay, I know not, my love—'twas she approach'd.

TAI   Behold thou, Cher, how Amber is array'd—
        Is't not the dress that thou wore yesterday?

CHER   [*to Amber:*] O, Ambular.

AMBER   —Good even, precious Cher.

CHER   Hast thou been ambling through my laundry, friend?   40

AMBER   As if! As if I'd ever copy thee,
          As if thou art the paragon of style,
          As if thy clothes are aught to be desir'd,

	As if I'd wear a rag from Judy's Shoppe!	
CHER	Thou mayst require an ambulance anon—	45
	Dost thou prefer the label *fashion victim,*	
	Or merely this: *ensembly challengèd?*	
AMBER	Tut!	

[Amber walks aside.

CHER	[*to Tai:*] —What a clone! A poor one, too, in troth.	
TAI	I'll warrant thou look'st far more fetching in	
	That gown than ever she could.	
TRAVIS	[*approaching:*] —Ladies!	50
	Your drinks I've brought with swiftness utmost.	

[He brings drinks but spills
some on Cher's shoes.

CHER	Hast thou no manners, imp? These satin are!	
	I thank thee, Travis, for my ruin'd shoes:	
	Record it with your high and worthy deeds.	
TRAVIS	Apologies, I meant no damage.	55

[Cher and Tai walk aside. Travis follows.

CHER	Beg pardon, I must have a towel anon!	

[She finds a towel and dabs her shoes.

	[*To Travis:*] This cannot be repair'd—they are destroy'd.	
TRAVIS	A paltry sum to pay unto the	
	Gods who have given us this party!	
	If my blunder has offended thee,	60
	Soon Travis shall restore amends, Cher.	
	Wouldst care for these, my drugs most chronic?	
CHER	It is, methinks, the least that thou canst do.	
TRAVIS	Hurrrah! The party presseth onward.	
TAI	I bid thee, light the flame and we shall smoke.	65

[Travis lights a smoke.

CHER	[*to Tai:*] Behold, across the room! 'Tis Elton, dancing.	

Pretend that Travis humorously speaks.
> *[Tai laughs heartily. Travis tries to laugh, too.*

TRAVIS   Our merriment is yet a myst'ry.
            Remind me, Tai: why are we laughing?

TAI   I know naught, for there's nothing funny here.   70

TRAVIS   [*aside:*] A lass most wondrous, yet confounding.

ELTON   [*approaching:*] Good even, may I share the smoke with
                                                          thee?

SUMMER   My friends, let us play Scylla and Charybdis,
            The game that's better known as suck and blow.

ELTON   [*aside:*] The perfect chance for my romantic ruse,   75
            Wherewith I may catch Cher in an embrace.
> *[Summer brings a playing card to her mouth,
> sucks it to her lips, and approaches Travis.
> He sucks the card to his lips as Summer
> releases it. Travis passes the card to Tai,
> and Tai to Elton. Elton lets the card drop
> to the ground as his lips approach Cher's,
> and he kisses her heartily. All laugh.*

CHER   Thou common-kissing lout! Canst thou not suck?

DIONNE   [*screaming:*] Ay me, for pity!

CHER   —Dionne's voice doth call.
> *[Cher and Tai rush across the room to
> Dionne's side, where she watches in dismay
> as Lawrence shaves Murray's head.*

DIONNE   [*to Murray:*] What's this? Thou hadst but little wit in thy
            Bald crown when thou gav'st all thy hair away.   80
            By heaven, wherefore do this to thy pate?

MURRAY   Thereby I keep it real. Real is it kept.

DIONNE   [*to Cher:*] Behold what he hath done unto his pate!
            Canst thou believe his errant, ugly choice?

MURRAY	Look thou upon the head of Lawrence, here. 85
LAWRENCE	To shave one's pate doth feel as smooth as glass,
	Like one might fly, for closer is the air.
MURRAY	Thou lookest fine.
LAWRENCE	—As thou shalt, too, my mate.
DIONNE	Why carest thou what Lawrence thinks of thee?
	'Tis I who must upon thy visage look. 90
	Thou follow'st like a sheep, and hath been shorn!
	'Twas horribly mistaken, Murray, for
	What shall I do with thee, when thou look'st thus?
	Ere portraits for our mem'ry books are drawn,
	Thou hast transform'd thyself to a bald eagle? 95
	What shall I tell our future grandchildren?
	This is enow!
MURRAY	[*mocking:*] —Ha, ha, "this is enow!"
DIONNE	Wouldst thou play games, then?
MURRAY	[*mocking:*] —"Wouldst thou, then,
	play games?"
DIONNE	It seemeth I must call upon thy mother.
MURRAY	My mother? Nay! Thou shalt do no such thing. 100
LAWRENCE	Be still! Thou bald didst come forth from the womb—
	How can thy mother, then, reject thy look?
	[Cher and Tai leave them.
CHER	Alas, this is a tale as old as time—
	Last year, at our spring dance, 'twas also thus:
	She spent the afterparty in the bathroom. 105
TAI	Their argument did near destroy my buzz.
CHER	My buzz is buzz'd, gray matter truly bak'd.

Enter BALTHASAR *on balcony. All dance during the singing.*

BALTHASAR [*singing:*] 'Tis Saturday, and I do roll,
             My homies near, my spirit full,
             Some sixteen instruments do play,   110
             Unto the shore we make our way!
                 Roll with the homies, saucy jack!
                 Roll with the homies, sip the yak!
             My carriage is a hearty ride,
             The people gawk when I'm outside,   115
             No gang of rogues our joy reduce—
             My homies bear the dinner juice.
                 Roll with the homies, &c.

CHER   [*to Tai:*] Shall we bump into people presently,
             And rub our elbows with our pleasant peers?   120

TAI   Indeed! My elbows could some bumping take.

TRAVIS   Yet Tai, wait thou for me, I prithee—
                         [*Cher walks aside. Travis jumps down
                             from a table toward Tai but falls.*

TAI   Art thou well, Travis? 'Twas a mighty fall.

TRAVIS   [*to other students:*] Why caught ye not my falling body?
             Your hospitality is wanting.   125

TAI   Thy leap—it was amazing, by my troth.
             I wish I could so leap, with courage rare.

TRAVIS   Nay, imitate me not, I prithee.

TAI   Yet wherefore should I not?

TRAVIS   —If thou didst—
             If women ev'rywhere went leaping,   130
             What would we lads do to impress them?

TAI   I know not. Stuff and things.

TRAVIS   —What stuffthings?
                         [*Cher notices Tai and Travis talking.*

CHER   [*aside:*] One tiny moment have I turn'd my head,

And she hath taken up again with Travis!
[*Approaching:*] Tai, thou art needed on the instant.
Come! 135
[She pulls Tai away from Travis.
Travis walks aside.
Behold, thy suitor Elton yonder sits,
His rhythmic body bobbing to the song,
Surrounded by his friends and confidantes.
[Cher and Tai dance together.

BALTHASAR   [*singing:*] The spices wrapp'd in paper fine,
Set it alight, and make it thine,   140
Pass to thy neighbor, share delight—
The night, forsooth, turns dynamite!
Roll with the homies, &c.

ELTON   [*aside:*] Behold the dazzling Cher as she doth dance,
Was ever beauty captur'd in a form?   145
She's like a statue, carv'd from purest stone,
Whose shapely curves do mark a master's touch.

CHER   [*aside:*] There's Elton, gazing our direction. Ha!
He is enamor'd of the lovely Tai.
My plan hath work'd; the two shall be a match.   150
[A student accidentally kicks off their
shoe, hitting Tai in the head.
O, Tai, art well? Pray, Elton, bring thine aid.

ELTON   To give thee service is my privilege.
[Elton picks up Tai and lays her on a table.

TRAVIS   [*approaching:*] Thou shouldst put ice upon her bruis'd
pate.

CHER   The situation's under our control.
Why dost thou bother us? Thou art not needed.   155

TRAVIS   Tai, art thou well? I bid thee, wake up.

CHER   She'd want thee to rejoin the revelers,
            Thou hast no place beside her—get thee hence.

TRAVIS   [*aside:*] Harumph. Mine aid she'd gladly welcome.
                            [*Travis walks aside, disconsolate.*

CHER   [*to Elton:*] If she doth lie unconscious, thou must help 160
            Her consciousness regain by asking questions,
            Which she may answer, keeping her awake.

ELTON   [*aside:*] How did I come to be in this position?
            'Tis not this lass whom I would have before
            Me, prone upon the table needing me.   165
            [*To Tai:*] What is the product of two sevens, eh?

CHER   Nay, ask thou just what she already knows.
                            [*Tai sits up and hits her head on a
                            lamp hanging above the table.*

ELTON   The situation goes from bad to worse.
            Thou hast a nasty bump upon thy head.

TAI   In sooth.

ELTON   —Shall we return to party's glow?   170

TAI   Yea, let us go.

ELTON   —Art sure? Canst thou do this?
                            [*He motions with his hand,
                            mimicking a rolling ocean wave.*
            [*Singing:*] Roll with the homies, saucy jack!
                            [*Tai makes the same motion.*

TAI   [*singing:*] Roll with the homies, saucy jack!

ELTON   Ha, thou art ready now! We'll thither go.
                            [*Tai and Elton return to the party together.*

CHER   [*aside:*] I must give credit where 'tis justly due, 175
            And in this instance credit falls to me.
            Such acts of mercy I bring to the world,
            Such deeds of goodness and philanthropy,

That love doth flourish, is ubiquitous.
Though I may be alone, my happiness   180
For Tai is like a lover's warm embrace.
'Tis like the book I read whilst in ninth grade,
Which was the best of times, the worst of times.
The volume's author, in his wisdom, writ:
"It is a far, far better thing to do   185
Some stuff for other people." Something like.

      Enter a MESSENGER, *who speaks with*
        CHER *briefly and then exits.*

A message cometh from my father, who
Sans doubt doth wonder where the time hath gone,
Since I am past my curfew by some hours.
He doth not realize that this outfit grants   190
No opportunity to wear a timepiece with't—
To dress in clocks would clock me out of fashion.
Of course, he doth not know where I have gone,
For I told him a tale of some deceit:
That I was venturing out with my mates   195
To wander hence and have a snack withal.
Belike his fears by now are taking root
As he doth wonder whether I have gone
To some far country for a simple meal.
Perchance, if I do not return anon,   200
He shall grow sick with worry. Daughter rude!
Home, then, to halt his fatherly concern—
In twenty minutes if I leave at once,
For Father saith e'er that ev'ry point
Within Los Angeles may be attain'd   205

	In only twenty minutes' carriage ride.
	I shall ask Elton; he shall take me home.
	[She approaches Elton and Tai.
	[*To Elton:*] Wouldst thou, I prithee, take me home again?
ELTON	'Twould be a pleasure to give thee a ride.
CHER	Apologies to take thee early hence, 210
	For thou, I'll wager, sooner wouldst remain.
	The ones who brought me, Dionne and her Murray,
	Are caught deep in the drama of the night,
	And argue all the while o'er this and that.
	She loves the part of hapless paramour. 215
	[Cher, Tai, and Elton begin to
	leave and encounter Summer.
	Holla, kind Summer. Was this party not
	A lovely—e'en if somewhat random—gath'ring?
SUMMER	Need'st thou a ride, Cher? I am leaving, too.
ELTON	Nay, I shall take her. 'Tis no bother, Summer.
SUMMER	My route shall take me near to Wilshire where 220
	It intersects with Linden. Art thou near?
TAI	'Tis close to where I live, above Olympic.
ELTON	Thou, Tai, then go with Summer presently,
	Whilst I deliver Cher unto her home.
CHER	[*aside:*] Nay, what is Elton doing? What a dolt— 225
	He sabotages his own chance to woo.
	[*To Summer:*] Take Wilshire unto Cannon, which doth turn
	To Benedict.
ELTON	—Nay, then she would go south,
	Whilst my course turns already to the north.
CHER	Thou couldst take Tai as thou to Sunset goest. 230
ELTON	Beyond all sense art thou, for then I would

Be forc'd to leave the freeway, which I hate—
Once on such wide and speedy boulevards,
Who'd give them up to drive a country lane?
Tai, go with Summer—Cher, come thou with me.   235
        [Tai climbs into Summer's carriage, and they
             exeunt. Exeunt all students and Balthasar
                    as Cher and Elton get into his carriage.

CHER   [*aside:*] If this is love, I comprehend it not—
Why take such pains to go with me when Tai
Is palpably the source of his affection?
I'll question him of her, to help him see
The error of his actions. [*To Elton:*] Did not Tai   240
Look most adorable this eventide?

ELTON   [*singing:*] Turn thou away, turn thou away,
        Heigh, heigh!

CHER   Her hair is lovely when 'tis wild and free,
As if it were the mane of lioness—   245
Yet also pretty when 'tis up and bound,
With curly tendrils peeking round the sides,
As in the drawing which adorns thy locker.

ELTON   Know'st that thou, Cher, art one of my best friends?
'Tis strange, since normally I do not have   250
Companions of thy sex.

CHER   —Then am I glad,
Because thy happiness means much to me.

ELTON   Does it?

CHER   —Indeed. I saw how hard it was
When thou and thy Folette were rent asunder;
Methought, perchance, thy heart would never heal.   255

ELTON   I'll wager we both know the feeling that
Ariseth when long loneliness prevails.

CHER   Whate'er thy meaning, prithee know thou this:
            'Twould make me glad to see thee settl'd soon.

ELTON   [*aside:*] Her meaning is as bold as sunlight's glow—   260
            And clear as bluest sky sans clouds of gray.
            I'll pull us over and fulfill my quest
            To woo her, kiss her, touch her, what you will.
                      [*He steers his carriage to the side of the road.*

CHER   Why have we stopp'd? Hath something gone awry?

ELTON   I knew 'twas true, and have for many weeks.   265
                      [*He tries to kiss her and she pushes him aside.*

CHER   Thou knewest what, thou too-familiar knave?

ELTON   I know that thou art well-nigh dead for me.

CHER   [*aside:*] This folly must be drunkenness, in troth,
            And therefore may I hope that it belongs
            But to the passing hour. [*To Elton:*] I'm much
                                              astonish'd— 270
            These words to me! Thou take me for a friend,
            So any message unto Tai I shall
            Be happy to deliver for thy sake,
            But no more of this unto me, I pray.

ELTON   To Tai? I have no word or thought for her.   275

CHER   Her picture doth adorn thy locker's wall.

ELTON   Thy picture doth adorn my locker's wall,
            Which thou didst paint, by thine own skillful hand.

CHER   Alas, this foul experience reminds
            Me of what they encounter'd at Twin Peaks.   280

ELTON   I knew thy heart was won when I kiss'd thee,
            Thou suck'd my soul t'ward thee, didst blow my mind.
                      [*He tries to kiss her a second time
                        and she pushes him aside again.*

CHER   Nay, suck and blow is only made for sport—

	It doth not signify the heart's desire.	
ELTON	Yea, we shall have some sport anon, indeed.	285

> [*He tries to kiss her a third time and
> she pushes him aside once more.*

CHER	Stop, stop! Before I brand thee villain, stop!	
ELTON	If thou wouldst have it so, I shall surcease,	
	Yet verily I do not understand:	
	Thou flirtest with me ev'ry day of th'year—	
CHER	As if! As if I ever cross'd that line,	290
	As if I ever thought of thee that way,	
	As if my conduct e'er was less than pure,	
	As if my friendliness hath turn'd to flirt!	
	I have, these past few weeks, tried earnestly	
	To tie thee unto Tai.	
ELTON	—Tai? Even so?	295
	Say wherefore I should e'en consider Tai.	
CHER	Nay, wherefore not?	
ELTON	—Canst thou be serious?	
	Know'st thou my father and his prominence?	
CHER	This is thine answer? Art so fill'd with pride?	
	Thou art too cramm'd with snobbery by half.	300
ELTON	I shall speak simply, that thou mayst hear truth:	
	Tai and myself—the phrase, e'en, makes me gag—	
	Are not a pair that maketh any sense.	
	I am a raging fire, and she still water,	
	I am the very heights, and she the depths,	305
	I am ocean, she a trifling drip,	
	I am a shooting star, and she but dirt.	
	However, when I think of thee and me,	
	It is a pair as like as peas and carrots.	
CHER	[*aside:*] O, misery, this was not what I plann'd.	310

> *[He tries to kiss her a fourth time*
> *and she pushes him aside again.*

      I bid thee, cease!

ELTON   —Relax, I pray.

CHER   —Nay, stop!

> *[She dismounts from the carriage.*

ELTON   Cher, prithee, do return. We'll be friends first.
           Where art thou bound? Thou hurtest but thyself—
           Wouldst thou walk home and catch a cold, or worse?
           Climb back into the carriage instantly!   315

CHER   Be gone! I do not wish thy company.

ELTON   If 'tis thy wish, then Elton flies anon.

> *[Exit Elton in his carriage.*

CHER   Nay, nay, where art thou going? Fie upon't!
           I want him not, yet would not be alone.
           My trouble grows like flowers in new soil,   320
           For I, as yet, am many miles from home.
           If this is what doth come of matchmaking,
           I swear I'll never play the sport again.
           This night hath shown me, if I doubted, that
           A girl can get burn'd when she plays with matches.   325
           Would that I had another ride. I could
           Attempt to hail a coach to take me home,
           Which, mayhap, would prove best and fastest, too.

> *Enter a* BANDIT.

BANDIT   Be still, and give me all thy valuables—
           Thou art a wealthy woman, I thy thief.   330
           Thy satchel and the ducats in thy purse,
           All shall be mine, or I shall work thee woe.

	Lie now upon the ground with thy face down.	
	Make haste, for patience is unknown to me.	
CHER	Thou dost not understand, sir. My new gown	335
	Was made by Azzedine Alaïa, who	
	Is known throughout the world for artistry,	
	Sophisticated style, and fashion high.	
BANDIT	The name's unknown and immaterial,	
	No matter the material A-what-a	340
	Doth use or how much thy kind worship him.	
CHER	Yet his designs are totally important!	

[The bandit brandishes a pistol.

BANDIT	I'll totally shoot thee where thou dost stand.	
	Thy pretty head doth not come near my conscience,	
	For 'tis thy wealth for which I've hither come.	345
	Down now, upon thy belly in a trice!	

[Cher lies facedown, whimpering.

	'Tis well thou art a lass accommodating.	
	Count thou unto one hundred as I go,	
	And thanks to thee for simple thievery.	

[Exit Bandit.

CHER	One, two, three, four—the rogue is gone at last.	350
	This evening turneth to a royal mess,	
	Harass'd and robb'd, my schemes undone at once.	
	Would that I could bid Dionne come for me,	
	Yet she is still with Murray at the fest.	
	My father—I could send a message thither—	355
	Yet he will be enrag'd if he doth know.	
	One person doth remain, whom I may call,	
	Yet his disdain shall shame me horribly.	

Enter JOSH *with* HEATHER, *in a carriage.*

JOSH	Holla, Cher? 'Tis an odd coincidence.
CHER	Josh, art thou busy?
HEATHER	—Who's this lady, Josh? 360
JOSH	'Tis Cher, the daughter of my stepfather.
	[*To Cher:*] Why art thou here, Cher?
CHER	—I was at a party,
	And left with one who should convey me home
	Yet rather did attempt to strike at me.
	His carriage I departed instantly, 365
	And he deserted me most cruelly.
	Another man, a bandit, then appear'd
	To take of me whatever he did please
	Whilst brandishing his pistol in my face.
	My ducats, satchel, ev'rything he took, 370
	Then yell'd at me as if I were a slave,
	Bade me to lie upon the filthy ground,
	And forc'd me to destroy my precious gown.
JOSH	For this—thine imposition on my night,
	Which I had plann'd to spend alone with Heather— 375
	Thou shalt owe me the world. Dost understand?
CHER	Indeed. My humble thanks for mercy giv'n.

>   [*Cher climbs into the carriage*
>   *with Josh and Heather.*

HEATHER	As I was saying, ere this interruption,
	The man is utterly ridiculous.
	He hath no single thought unique inside 380
	His puny, insignificant, weak brain.
JOSH	Methinks there merit is in learning form
	At once.
HEATHER	—Josh, prithee tell: art thou in jest?
	He taketh our young minds at their most fecund

	And doth restrain them ere they wander through	385
	The luscious, fruitful garden of ideas.	
	'Tis just as, famously, once Hamlet said:	
	"To thine own self be true."	

CHER   —Nay, 'twas not Hamlet.

HEATHER   My memory of Hamlet is complete—
          Erratic, sometimes, are my recollections,   390
          Though not in this case. I know *Hamlet* well,
          And saw it at the Globe the other day.

CHER   My mem'ry of Mel Gibson is complete—
          The actor who did take the noble part—
          And 'twas not he who spake the words thou us'd.   395
          Those words were spoken by Polonius.

*   [Josh laughs, and Heather glares at him.*

JOSH   [*aside:*] By all that's marvelous, young Cher is right,
          Yet Heather is too full of arrogance
          T'admit defeat. Cher ever doth surprise—
          Just when I think her shallow, base, and dumb,   400
          She shows a depth that I could not predict.

*   [They arrive at Heather's residence.*

          [*To Cher:*] I shall walk Heather to the door. Wait here,
          And keep thou clear of trouble's spacious path.

*   [Josh and Heather walk to her door*
*   and embrace while Cher looks on.*

CHER   Behold the lovers playing their sweet scene,
          Josh kissing Heather with a passion rare   405
          Whilst she responds with amorous intent.
          I should be happy for them, should I not?
          Yet as I watch them, I feel only bleak,
          As if disaster knock'd upon my door
          Presenting horrors unknown hitherto—   410

E'en worse than what they face in Malibu.

> *[Exit Heather. Josh returns to the carriage*
> *and they drive on in silence. Exeunt.*

ACT III

SCENE 1

Bronson Alcott High School and Westside Pavilion mall.

Enter BALTHASAR *on balcony.*

BALTHASAR [*singing:*] The angels fall like rain,
                   And love is heaven's way,
                   Inside thee is time's gain,
                   Which never fades away.
                          The ghost in thee   5
                          Shall never fade,
                          See hey and lackaday.
                   The race, it hath begun,
                   And I am on thy side.
                   Would that it had been won,   10
                   But thou hast stopp'd the ride.
                          The ghost in thee
                          Shall never fade,
                          See hey and lackaday.
                   O, let us run away,   15
                   My mood doth yearn for thee,
                   The stars shall come to play,
                   Whilst I do burn for thee.
                          The ghost in thee
                          Shall never fade,   20
                          See hey and lackaday.

                                        [Exit Balthasar.

Enter CHER.

CHER   I knew not what to say to Tai today—
My nerves were fraught with fear and desolation.
Yea, even Fabian, my strong masseuse
Reported to me—as she rubb'd me down—   25
She felt the tension growing in my back.
When finally I broke the news to Tai,
She was as desolate as I expected,
Self-loathing mix'd up with despondency.

Enter TAI *and* DIONNE.

TAI   He doth despise my hips, is this not so?   30
DIONNE   Nay, 'tis not so, for thou art beautiful,
Thy hips, thy lips, thy parts all pure perfection.
CHER   The lad is utter foolishness itself.
Thou shalt do better yet, mark thou my words.
DIONNE   He hath a head as large as any town,   35
So full of his own import is the boy,
If it is pride thou wantest in a man,
Thou canst no better do than Elton, yea,
Yet if thou wouldst seek someone who shall love,
Adore, and treasure thee, he's not for thee.   40
Thou art well rid of him.
CHER   —Indeed, he thinks
He is a gift from God to mortal women.
DIONNE   Too good by twice—
CHER   —Nay, thrice!
DIONNE   —Art thou for him.
TAI   Thy logic, friends, but wishful thinking seems.
If I'm too good for him, by twice or thrice,   45
It follows I could have him twice or thrice—

Some two or three sweet Eltons in my life—
Yet I have zero, infinitely fewer,
Not e'en one Elton I can call mine own.
If your words had a jot of truth to them,   50
Would I, at least, not be with one of him?

DIONNE   [aside:] Alas, her logic's irrefutable.

CHER   An idea cometh o'er me like a wave.
We shall our next class purposely avoid
And wander happily unto the mall.   55
Therein we'll have a fest of calories
And view the latest Christian Slater play,
Wherein he is a lawyer who doth serve
A man accus'd of murder in the first.
Soon Elton shall be but a memory—   60
Food, friends, and fun shall take thy mind therefrom.

TAI   You two are better friends than I could hope—
So sweet and tender, caring and concern'd.

                                    [They all embrace.

CHER   Let us, then, to the mall with utmost haste!

They walk to the mall and sit down at a restaurant.
Enter various WAITERS *and* DINERS.

DIONNE   We'll dine here, for the meat is plenty fresh—   65
I mean the waiters, they who are a feast
For hungry eyes and rav'nous appetites.
See that one there, whose flesh is taut and sleek—
Were he serv'd unto me, I'd eat each bite.

TAI   Yea, share a piece with me—there is enow.   70
Methinks he is a banquet fit for two.

CHER   As you survey him, what do you conclude?

TAI	I would not put him out my chamber doors.
DIONNE	On second glance, he is unduly small;
	The man for Dionne shall be bulkier. 75
CHER	Nay, many muscles are not to my taste—
	I like a thinner cut, a finer morsel.
TAI	My palate is not so refin'd as yours—
	Be it a man, I'll sample its delights.
	One circumstance, though, slayeth ev'ry craving; 80
	Should someone's manhood be a warpèd one—
	An 'twere a shepherd's crook or bishop's crosier—
	I'd gladly fast ere sup with such a one.
CHER	Thy meaning is a mystery to me.
	A shepherd's crook or bishop's crosier—what? 85
	Methought we spoke in dining metaphors,
	But thou hast ta'en a most pastoral turn.
DIONNE	I bid thee, Tai, don't frighten our poor Cher.
TAI	What words of horror said I? Friends, if I
	Misspoke, you have my deep apologies. 90
DIONNE	Our Cher doth save herself for someone more—
	Sir Luke of Perry or his noble kind.
TAI	Thou art a virgin, Cher? Impossible!
CHER	Thou say'st the word as if it were a curse,
	A spell to place a pox on humankind, 95
	Or incantation from a witch's mouth:
	"Fillet of virgin, in the cauldron boil
	And bake, with eye of newt and toe of frog!"
TAI	Use not the vulgar label *virgin*, please.
	The modern and correct phrase thou must use 100
	Is *hymenally challeng'd*, verily.
CHER	There is no rush to break the bonds asunder,
	And cast away my maidenhead thereby.

Ye know how choosy I can be of shoes,
And they must only circumscribe my feet.   105
I wait upon a man whom I can love,
The person who shall earn the right to Cher.
Does Cher a mighty, noble man deserve?
Does Cher a witty, thoughtful man desire?
Does Cher a simple, honest man pursue?   110
Does Cher a fun, if foolish, man require?
If thou wouldst plumb my depths, start with "Does
                                                    Cher?"

TAI   Such depths thou hast, that none may call thee shallow.

CHER   Thou, Dee, art hypocritical, in troth.

TAI   Wait, thou and Murray never did the deed?   115
              Assum'd I you were making the beast with
              Two backs, so strong is your relationship.

DIONNE   My lad is satisfied, and hath no cause
              For frustrated complaint. Yet, technic'lly,
              I am a virgin yet, and there's an end.   120
              When I do speak of ends, ye catch my drift.

TAI   [*aside:*] Her drift hath pass'd directly o'er my head.

              Enter BALTHASAR *on balcony.*

BALTHASAR   [*singing:*] 'Tis Saturday, and I do roll,
              My homies near, my spirit full,
              Some sixteen instruments do play,   125
              Unto the shore we make our way!
                  Roll with the homies, saucy jack!
                  Roll with the homies, sip the yak!

TAI   Alack!

CHER   —What? Art unwell? What is it, Tai?

TAI	The music! Listen, for our song is sung—	130
	That unto which sweet Elton and I danc'd.	
CHER	Poor flower petal, we cannot protect	
	Thy heart from ev'ry quaver, clef, and staff.	
TAI	[*singing:*] Roll with the homies, saucy jack!	

[Tai begins to cry. Exit Balthasar.

DIONNE	Brave Tai, thy tears are but a foofaraw,	135
	Although, sans doubt, it matters much to thee.	
TAI	Apologies, my friends. If I could rid	
	Myself of these unpleasant memories	
	By banging of my pate upon the table,	
	I'd gladly try it. Yea, mayhap I should!	140

[She slams her head on the table a few
times, until Dionne stops her.

DIONNE	Stop, prithee, Tai! Grief makes thee overwrought.	
	Come with me, to the bathroom, where we shall	
	Make thee once more presentable and calm.	
	Cher, we shall meet thee back at school again.	

[Exeunt Dionne and Tai.
Cher walks back to school.

CHER	Tai's mourning period is not yet o'er,	145
	And may yet be consid'rable in length.	
	Unless, perchance, I wade into the waters	
	Of matchmaking to quickly fill her void.	
	I'll peradventure find another lad	
	To take the place of Elton in a trice.	150
	Yet who? For as I think upon my peers—	
	Though I'd not be a traitor to my age,	
	No turncoat to my generation bold—	
	I do confess confusion and dismay.	
	The way lads dress is nothing short of odd,	155

As if they fell, like apples, from their beds,
Adorn'd themselves in poorly fitting pants—
More like broad bags than pantaloons, in troth—
Then cover greasy hair with filthy caps,
Which they wear backward and proclaim it style.   160
In public they appear array'd as such,
And should we women swoon to see them so?
Nay, I think not, and never shall be sway'd!
To search for lads in high school is a quest
As useless as the hunt for meaning in   165
The dramas of the actor Pauly Shore—
The nation's jester: a most dull fool he,
And none but libertines delight in him.

She sits down in her classroom. Enter MASTER WENDELL
HALL *and various* STUDENTS *including* DIONNE, TAI, MURRAY,
ELTON, *and* AMBER. *Enter* CHRISTIAN *with a flourish.*

[*Aside:*] By all that's marvelous, a handsome lad!

HALL   [*to Christian:*] Thou, then, art the elusive Christian,
                               yea? 170

CHRISTIAN   Most happily shall I assume my seat,
                If thou shalt tell me whither I am bound.

HALL   One seat, third back, beyond where Cher doth sit.

CHER   [*aside:*] Though I should find a newfound mate for Tai,
                What is thy harm in searching for myself?   175
                Lads are in surplus far above demand.
                   [*She intentionally knocks a quill from her desk.*

CHRISTIAN   [*aside:*] A chick doth signal me by feather shed.
                Perchance she'll help me climb the pecking order.
                         [*He picks up the quill.*

           [*To Cher:*] Thy legs are wondrous long and passing
                                       smooth.

CHER   My thanks—thy gaze is long, thy words are smooth.   180

HALL   Cher?

CHER   —Present.

HALL   —Yea, so 'twas establishèd
           When first I took th'attendance of the class.
           'Tis time, now, for thine oral.

CHER   —Pardon me?

HALL   Thine oral on a theme original—
           Thou chosest violence in the media.   185

CHER   Of course!

                  [*She walks to the front of the classroom.*

HALL   [*aside:*]   —What did she think I meant by oral?
           Indeed, what did ye think, O audience?

CHER   Behold: th'attorney general doth say
           Too much of violence doth appear within
           Our stages, halls, and entertainment venues.   190
           I do agree, and tell ye it must stop.
           Yet e'en if ev'ry violent show were stopp'd,
           Would there not be reports of cruelty,
           Oppression, murder, and injustices?
           Until humanity so peaceful grows   195
           That violence hath no part in daily life,
           Why should it from our entertainment flee?
           Is not our art reflection of our lives,
           Or was it th'other way around? Ah, well,
           Whatever 'tis, ye have heard mine opinion.   200
           My thanks for your attention and respect.

                                    [*All applaud.*

HALL   Hath anyone a comment? Elton, thou?

ELTON	My foot is sore. May I unto the nurse?
HALL	Thou, Travis? Any comment on Cher's speech?
TRAVIS	Two thumbs enthusiastic'lly rais'd— 205
	Fine holiday fun for the fam'ly.
AMBER	Art serious? Was't I alone who heard
	The words that pour'd forth from Cher's bumbling lips?
	Methought her speech gave off a horrid stench,
	As if a rotting corpse had crawl'd inside 210
	Her mind, releasing odors from her mouth.
CHER	Mayhap the smell thy nose hath lately smell'd
	Was that of thine own faux-designer perfume.

[The bell rings. All exeunt except
Cher, Amber, and Christian.

CHRISTIAN	[*to Cher:*] Thy speech did hit the mark—a perfect hit.

[Exeunt Cher and Christian.

AMBER	In sooth, she always hath the final word, 215
	Although she is a shallow, stupid girl.
	Humiliating me is her vocation,
	And always doth she have the upper hand.
	Though I would ne'er admit to such a thought,
	How I do wish I could be more like Cher. 220
	She is ador'd by all whom she encounters,
	Belovèd of both teachers and our peers,
	With wealth enow to comfortable be,
	And garments in the latest, highest style.
	She calls me a pretender, for I am— 225
	Not popular or treasur'd like she is,
	Adorn'd in clothing that doth fashion ape.
	Forgive me, for I never shall be Cher,
	Mere Amber, lacking love and full of care.

[Exit.

SCENE 2

Bronson Alcott High School and the Horowitz house.

Enter CHER. *Enter* CHRISTIAN *severally, watching her from afar.*

CHER   [*aside:*] The past few days were spent in careful schemes,
              Performing those deeds any lass would do:
              Adoring letters sent I to myself,
              And open'd them with glee in Christian's sight.
              Bouquets of flowers did arrive for me,   5
              Which came from no fond suitor but myself.
              A box of choc'lates came, which I did share
              With students in my class, and Christian, too—
              Whatever can be done to draw attention
              Unto one's mouth is strategy well play'd.   10
              My ploy was perfect, cunning in the height,
              For by it I appear'd much in demand,
              Desir'd by ev'ryone throughout the school—
              If, by some chance, the lad did not yet know.
              Occasionally, I would doff my vest   15
              To show the alabaster skin beneath,
              Thereby announcing, like a prancing bird,
              My willingness to find a fitting mate.
              This tactic makes lads think of nakedness,
              Which doth excite the humors terribly   20
              And calls to mind the act of sex itself.
CHRISTIAN   [*approaching:*] Good morning, duchess.
CHER   —Yea? Dost thou mean me?
CHRISTIAN   Hast thou some weekend plans for merriment?

	Belike thou plann'st a ration of a'rashin'?	
CHER	What?	
CHRISTIAN	—I am new here, yet methought thou might	25
	Know where the best of parties shall be held,	
	Where clams are bak'd with perfect sauce atop	
	And kids are bak'd in saucy, clammy tops.	
CHER	My ex-stepbrother's friends do plan a fest.	
	Thou mayst go with me, if it pleaseth thee.	30
CHRISTIAN	I would; it shall. 'Tis settl'd—we've a date.	

                     [Exit Christian. Cher walks to her house.

CHER	My afternoon I'll spend in preparation	
	To go with Christian to the gathering.	
	My pretty, new white gown I'll wear tonight,	
	Which shall turn Christian's eyes and heart to me.	35

                             [She changes clothes.

Meanwhile, my father hath an urgent case
That needeth his attention right away.

Enter MEL HOROWITZ, JOSH, *and various* CLERKS, *working.*

Our house becomes a rowdy lawyers' den,
With clerks and Josh assisting his pursuit.
Through some gazillion depositions they   40
Are reading, thus to learn how they may win.

                            [A bell rings.

[*To Mel:*] I prithee Father, open thou the door!
'Twill not be me to answer—he must wait!
'Twas ever thus when suitors come to call.

MEL	He, then, shall wait outside. I'll answer not.	45
CHER	Josh, prithee, wilt thou welcome Christian in?	
	Delay no longer, please—I beg of thee!	

                                      [Exit Cher in haste.

JOSH   [*aside:*] Her whining would make angels grind their
                                                        teeth—
            It pierceth silence like a needle's point.
            To quiet her is worth the few steps' journey.   50

                    JOSH *opens the door of the house.*
                    Enter CHRISTIAN *with a flourish.*

CHRISTIAN   What is the hap?
                                      [Josh removes Christian's hat
                                            and hands it to him.

JOSH   —She is not yet prepar'd.
CHRISTIAN   [*to Mel:*] Ho, man. This pile of bricks thou hast is nice—
            Thou must be wealthy, or just fortunate.
MEL   Art thou a drinking man?
CHRISTIAN   —Nay, I am well.
            Thine offer, though, is truly generous.   55
MEL   'Twas not an offer for a spirit, lout—
            I merely ask if thou drink'st alcohol.
            Think'st thou I would give liquor to a teen
            Who soon shall drive my daughter in his carriage?
            I'd rather place my foot upon a stump   60
            And hack it off withal a dull-edg'd axe.
CHRISTIAN   I do receive thy most protective vibe—
            Thou givest me a shovel, and I dig.
MEL   What is the matter? What doth ail thee, lad?
            Thy manner shows no marks of sanity.   65
            Perhaps thou dost imagine that the death
            Of Sammy Davis left an opening
            Within the Rat Pack's ranks, and thou art bound

T'audition for his place? It is not so—
Thy look, thy style, thine attitude doth reek   70
Of all that holds ye younger people back.
Thou art the very emblem of disgrace,
Exemplar of a nation's disappointment.

Enter CHER, *dressed finely.*

JOSH   [*aside:*] O beauty, did I know thy name e'er now?
CHER   Good even, Christian.
CHRISTIAN   —Dollface, look at thee!   75
CHER   Thou art as handsome as the day is long.
                              [*They kiss cheeks.*
CHRISTIAN   Ne'er was there artist who could capture thee,
              No sculptor who could cast thy perfect frame,
              Ne'er a composer who could sing thy notes,
              No writer who, with words, could thee describe.   80
              Thou stunning art, past human comprehension.
JOSH   [*aside, to Mel:*] Shalt thou let her go yonder, so array'd,
              As if her name were Eve, her gown a fig leaf?
MEL   Cher, come thou hither presently, I pray.
CHER   What is it, Father?
MEL   —Say, by heav'n or hell,   85
              What is that cloth—or lack thereof—thou wear'st?
CHER   'Tis but a dress.
MEL   —O? As defin'd by whom?
CHER   The dictionary writ by Calvin Klein.
MEL   Mayhap 'tis underwear; 'tis not a gown.
              Go thou upstairs and something don atop,   90
              That thou mayst cover'd and more modest be.
CHER   Already 'twas my plan. Wait thou a moment.

[Exit Cher.

MEL   [*to Christian:*] Thou, boy! Should anything befall my
                                                                daughter,
             I have a musket and a shovel both,
             And happily would I the pair employ.   95
             Methinks no one would mourn thee, wert thou gone.
CHRISTIAN   [*aside:*] No parent was so charming since Medea.

Enter CHER, *wearing the same dress and a see-through sweater.*

CHER   Farewell, sweet father.
CHRISTIAN   —Gentlemen, adieu.
                            [Cher and Christian walk aside,
                                    heading to the party.
JOSH   [*aside:*] My plan hath gone awry, and she is gone.
             I cannot fathom wherefore I am irk'd—   100
             I care not how the lass comports herself.
                            [Mel, Josh, and clerks continue to work
                            as Cher and Christian venture outside.
CHER   Thy carriage is as fancy as can be!
CHRISTIAN   My thanks. Thy father's scary as can be.
CHER   Indeed.
                            [They climb into Christian's carriage.
CHRISTIAN   —Dost thou like Billie Holiday?
CHER   He is the greatest singer ever known.   105

Enter BALTHASAR *on balcony.*

BALTHASAR   [*aside:*] Who do you think shall wander into town?
                You never shall guess who—
                'Tis lovable, huggable Em'ly Brown,

      Or Lady Brown to you.

      If e'er the rainfall, pattering, comes down,   110

         My heaven turneth blue—

      Can it be sending me that Em'ly Brown

         Or Lady Brown to you?

                 [Exit Balthasar. Exeunt Cher
                      and Christian severally.

JOSH   *[to Mel:]* I did not like the lad, nor never shall.

MEL   What is to like? He is an errant youth.   115

JOSH   Perchance I should unto the party go,

     That I may watch o'er Cher and keep her safe.

MEL   If thou bethinkest thou shouldst thither go,

     I will not hinder thee—go with my blessing.

JOSH   Thou hast no need of me?

MEL   —Nay, all is well.   120

JOSH   If thou preferest—

MEL   —Get thee hence, be gone!

JOSH   I shall. Mine eyes shall stand in place of thine,

     Observing Cher with keenest aptitude,

     So shall it be like thou wert there thyself.

MEL   Go, then, and may it bring thee reassurance.   125

                        [Exit Josh.

The lad's emotions wildly swirl about

As if she were the sea and he a squall.

One thing is certain—if I keep him here,

He shall be little use to anyone.

Let him go thither to the party where   130

He'll keep an eye upon my rosebud, Cher.

                        [Exeunt.

SCENE 3

The party.

Enter CHER, CHRISTIAN, JOSH, ELTON, AMBER,
many STUDENTS, *and few* ADULTS *at the party. Enter*
BALTHASAR *and other* MUSICIANS *on balcony.*

BALTHASAR A sonnet, young ones, to begin our fest:
     [*Singing:*] There was a place, whose name I did forget,
     Is't that I can't recall, or choose I not?
     Whate'er it be, it causeth me to fret,
     Yet let's continue, that we find the plot.   5
     There was a girl whose name I do not know.
     She gave affection; I with love did bind her.
     I told her if I left, one day I'd show—
     Perchance I shall, yet may need a reminder.
     There was a verse that I had hop'd to write— 10
     One day, a book entire I shall design.
     Someday, be it in daytime or at night,
     I would both be and spend a storyline.
     One day! One day! When it shall be, who knows?
     Someday, someday, yea someday I suppose. 15

          [All dance. Cher and Christian
           dance close to each other.

CHER   [*aside:*] We dance, and 'tis as though I have grown wings,
     Transported to the air upon a feather.
     Our bodies touch, and instantly my heart
     Begins to beat a march at double time,
     The thumping forceful such that all shall hear't. 20

I shall not call this nascent feeling love,
Lest it be spoil'd before it can mature.
Yet, if this be not foreshadow of love—
If my mind can be practically numb
And I forget all others but the lad,   25
If I feel I could walk upon the clouds,
Ascendant, like one walking with the gods,
If I can see his smile, his look, his moves,
And recognize therein a soul inclin'd,
Yet still this be not love—I'll never trust   30
My heart or its discerning pow'rs again.

Enter TAI, *who stumbles and falls as she walks in.*

	Alas, poor Tai! My sister, art thou well?	
TAI	Fie! 'Tis embarrassing as night is dark.	
CHER	Nay, none did see the fall that did befall.	
TAI	Thy words are full of friendship's comfort, aye,	35
	Yet I am certain thou art wrong. Forsooth,	
	I shall be known the night entire as she	
	Who hither came upon her derrière!	
CHER	I promise, Tai, no soul hath thee espied.	
STUDENT 1	[*approaching, to Tai:*] Say, art thou hurt? Thy fall look'd terrible—	40
	In all my days, I never saw a fall	
	That seem'd as painful as the one thou hadst.	
	I'd likely weep, should I go tumbling thus.	
TAI	My gratitude for thy concern, I'm sure.	

       [*Student 1 walks aside. Tai notices*
        Elton dancing with Amber.

     Cher, look—'tis Elton! He who haunts my dreams,   45

Caught dancing happily with Amber—ah!
Not only am I easily dismiss'd,
But he hath taken up with that foul trollop?

CHER   Belike he only dances with her, Tai,
And hath no thought of amorous intent.   50

[Elton and Amber kiss.

TAI   Pray, tell: think'st thou the lass is beautiful?

CHER   Were she a painting, she were a Monet.

TAI   Who is Monet?

CHER   —An artist of renown.
From far away, his paintings lovely look,
Yet closer in, the truth doth come to light—   55
A mess of splotches, blemishes, and strokes.
Let us ask Christian. [*To him:*] Say, what makest thou
Of Amber, what is thine opinion of her?

CHRISTIAN   She dwells in Hagsville. Population: one.

CHER   [*to Tai:*] The truth hath been reveal'd, from one who is 60
A connoisseur of women, verily.

CHRISTIAN   Wouldst thou believe the hosts of this event
Are charging for the priv'lege to drink beer?
Here is my charge: if thou wouldst lend a ducat,
I'll gladly pay you Tuesday for a beer   65
Today.

[Cher pulls money from her dress
and hands it to Christian.

CHER   —Of course. Charge it to mine account.
Return anon with beer, and we shall charge
Unto the dance floor.

CHRISTIAN   —Thank you heartily.

[Christian walks aside, to buy beer.
He talks with the barkeep.

TAI   He is adorable in the extreme!

CHER   Dost thou bear witness to his moving heart,   70
         How ev'ry day it closer turns to me,
         An 'twere a sunflower and I the sun?
         He's lim'd, I warrant you, past all defense.
         Another lass approacheth unto him
         And he ignores her like she were a pest—   75
         "Unhand me, harlot, Cher's the one for me."
         Thus says he, or so I imagine 'tis.
         He and the barkeep strike a conversation—
         It seems they do enjoy each other well.
         He peradventure tells the man of me   80
         And how he strives to win my tender heart.
         Mayhap the two shall soon become good friends,
         The barkeep our best man when we are wed.
                         [Tai sees Josh talking with a
                                man across the room.

TAI   Behold, there's Josh unto the party join'd!

CHER   I did not see him enter, yet his nature   85
         Cannot escape itself; he hath slunk in
         Unnotic'd to the party. Thereupon,
         Discovering the sole adult herein,
         He speaketh with the man excitedly.
         'Tis like he hath no sense of what fun is,   90
         Or—in the knowing—would destroy it wholly.
                         [Josh waves at Cher across the
                                room, and she waves back.

TAI   This jumper thou advisèd me to wear—
         Should it be tied around my waist, like such?
         Alas, I know not what the fashion is.

CHER   Around thy waist shall suit thy sleek ensemble,   95

	And leave the lads desiring more from thee.
CHRISTIAN	[*returning:*] Art ready, Cher? My feet await, prepar'd
	To set thy heels once more to frolicking.

[They return to the dance floor.

BALTHASAR	[*singing:*] Where didst thou go? Where didst thou go?
	Mine emptiness doth grow. 100
	Where didst thou go? Where didst thou go?
	I'm lost, and fain would know!
TAI	[*aside:*] Alone, once more, like an abandon'd dog,
	I stand with no one here to dance with me.
	Mine Elton holds another lass's arms, 105
	His gaze ne'er settl'd on me in the least—
	I am the last one pick'd, and always was.
	Sweet Cher, who call'd to me when I was new
	And e'er hath prov'd herself a loyal friend,
	Swings on the arm with Christian presently, 110
	Forsaking me—and who could blame her for't?
	Before I mov'd here, I was mis'rable:
	Few friends, and none on whom I could depend.
	My life, uprooted unto California,
	Seem'd desolate, with little cause for hope, 115
	'Til I met Cher and Dionne at our school
	And started to believe all would be well.
	They have been beacons in a stormy sea,
	Illuminating me with thoughtful care.
	Now, though, as I stand helpless and alone, 120
	The feelings of rejection rise once more,
	And make me feel uncertain and bereft.
	The men pass by, with glances, smirks, and frowns,
	Ne'er once considering me worthy of
	Attention, or a turn upon the floor. 125

CHER   [*aside:*] The merry band of minstrels is superb,
              The night near perfect, dancing with my lad—
              Fine Christian, most attractive man herein.
              Yet for a moment, happiness doth pause
              For there, across the room, I spy poor Tai,   130
              Who hath no partner in this happy dance.
                                        [*Josh approaches Tai.*

JOSH   Holla, Tai—wouldst thou dance with me awhile?
              We modern folk are far too still, methinks,
              Though nature hath created us to move.

CHER   [*aside:*] O, Josh—a miracle by heaven sent!   135
              He asketh Tai to dance, such chivalry!
              So sweet his action, I could kiss the man.
                              [*Josh and Tai begin dancing together.*
              [*To Christian:*] Behold, Josh hath ask'd Tai to dance
                                        with him—
              He never dances. Is it not delightful?

CHRISTIAN   His usual abstention hath its cause,   140
              For see how he doth jostle, flop, and lurch?

CHER   Nay, he hath come unto the lady's rescue,
              That she feel not deserted 'midst the fun.

CHRISTIAN   Thine eyes observe the charity I miss,
              Yet thou dost teach me rightly to perceive.   145
                              [*Cher waves at Josh across the
                                room, and Josh smiles at her.*

JOSH   [*aside:*] My vast humiliation while I dance—
              For I am most unskill'd, and know it well—
              Is worth the trouble for a smile from Cher,
              Which lighteth darkness like the blessèd moon.
              Behold, now, how her Christian danceth with   150
              A lad who slyly sidles next to him.

Is not that strange? Yet Cher doth notice not.
Perhaps I make too much of what I see—
These mountains are but molehills, certainly.

> *[All continue dancing. Exeunt some*
> *students as the music begins to fade. Cher,*
> *Josh, and Tai sit together, exhausted.*
> *Christian continues to dance.*

CHRISTIAN   [*aside:*] Until the final note of music plays,   155
Until the march of drum and fife doth cease,
Until I'm made to leave, I shall dance on.
Faeries, come take me out of this dull world,
For I would ride with you upon the wind,
Run on the top of the dishevel'd tide,   160
And dance upon the mountains like a flame.

> *[Christian continues to dance,*
> *talking with other lads.*

JOSH   How fare ye, Cher and Tai? For I can see
Some marks of red around your eyes, as though
Your bodies yearn for sleep thus far denied.

CHER   Although this night hath been a grand success,   165
With drowsiness success to excess turns.
I am prepar'd and eager to depart.

TAI   Exhaustion is the country where I dwell.

CHER   Let us hail Christian, that we may set forth.
[*To Christian:*] O, Christian, shall we hence? The hour
                                                    is late. 170

CHRISTIAN   E'en now? These friendly lads I chatted with
Have shar'd intelligence of th'afterparty,
Where music, dancing, and delight live on.

CHER   My trainer earlier in the morning comes.

JOSH   I shall take Cher and Tai home, whilst thou goest   175

	Upon thy merry way to parties new.
CHRISTIAN	I could not ask this of thee.
CHER	—Nay, stay thou—
	Thou art so young and full of joie de vivre,
	Thou shouldst not burden'd be by we two sloths.
CHRISTIAN	Ne'er came a sloth in fur as fine as thine.
	Art thou most certain?
CHER	—Stay, and seize the day.
CHRISTIAN	My thanks. I'll call upon thee on the morrow.

CHRISTIAN I could not ask this of thee.

CHER   —Nay, stay thou—
Thou art so young and full of joie de vivre,
Thou shouldst not burden'd be by we two sloths.

CHRISTIAN Ne'er came a sloth in fur as fine as thine. 180
Art thou most certain?

CHER   —Stay, and seize the day.

CHRISTIAN My thanks. I'll call upon thee on the morrow.

     [Exeunt Christian and some lads. Exeunt
      all other students as Cher, Josh, and Tai
      climb into Josh's carriage. Tai falls asleep.

CHER 'Twas passing decent that thou danc'd with Tai,
For she was lonesome and 'twas like thou wert
A knight who answereth a damsel's cry. 185

JOSH The pleasure was all mine—I am no knight,
A far cry from, but merely hop'd to make
Tai's night less damnable through answer'd need.

CHER Hast thou borne witness to a change in her,
Like night turn'd day?

JOSH   —Yea, 'neath thy tutelage, 190
A change in her is born, as she explores
The challenging domain of midriffs bare.
I riff thereon too much, perhaps, for with
Thy silence thou dost amply bear my challenge.
What of it, then? Wouldst thou not rather stay 195
And fill the night with thy main knight, e'en Christian?
Or, as I'd rather call him, Ring-a-Ding?

CHER Indeed, if, for a moment I believ'd
That Father would not ding me if I spent
A night with anyone before a ring 200

Appeareth on my finger. He shall be
Awake the whole night worrying o'er me,
If I do not return.

JOSH   —Yea, he'll not rest
Until the depositions are complete.

CHER   Let us do him some benefit, I pray—   205
An action dopious on both our parts—
And stop for food upon the pathway home,
That we my father's hunger may depose.
He and his many clerks have not, I'll wager,
Had aught to eat—they must be famishèd.   210

JOSH   Most dopious indeed—let us proceed
To part them from their gastronomic need.

                                              [*Exeunt.*

SCENE 4

The Horowitz house.

Enter MEL HOROWITZ *and* CLERKS.

MEL   [*aside:*] Mine appetite is bursting for a meal,
For cloudy grow the thoughts when one is tir'd.
Upsetting is each task in hunger's face,
And anger is the swift result thereof.
How can I focus on these depositions   5
Amidst the rumbling of mine abdomen,
The cries and moans of stomach most unfed?

There should some word exist that would describe
The way that hunger quickly doth advance
To anger. Yet what would be such a term, 10
Combining *anger* unto *hunger*, hmm?
If my mind were not caught in such a fog,
Disrupted by the lack of food below't,
Belike I could discover just the word—
Gerhunan? It doth start with growling sound, 15
The *grr* my belly maketh even now.
Anhunger? This doth ring with Cockney tones
And satisfieth not discerning ears.
Alas, the word escapes me vexingly—
I cannot think of it, which maketh angry! 20

Enter CHER *and* JOSH, *delivering food for the
clerks, which they begin eating voraciously.*

CHER   [*aside:*] This midnight feast is a phenomenon,
            Reviving all the lawyers' flagging moods!
MEL   Delicious meat to fill a belly bare,
            'Tis not mere beef, 'tis banquet of the gods,
            Which grants we humans immortality. 25
CHER   Nay, Father, thou must not ingest the meat,
            For it shall not thine arteries abet.
            The salad—eat the salad, for thy health!
MEL   Thou hast my gratitude for bringing this
            Much-needed banquet. Yet thou also earn'st 30
            My deep frustration by thy prohibition!
            Get hence, sweet daughter—let me eat, this once!
                    [*Exeunt Mel and clerks, eating. Josh and Cher
                    sit on a sofa together, listening to a music box.*

CHER   Though it shall seem unusual, sans doubt,
        Oft I have more enjoyment of a night
        In quiet entertainment, spent inside,   35
        Than at a party, dancing all the night.
        Belike 'tis that my festival attire
        Constricts my movements most uncomfortably.

JOSH   How many hours each day dost thou expend
        In grooming?

CHER   —Some are not as fortunate   40
        As thee, so natur'lly adorable.

JOSH   Cease, prithee, for thou causest me to blush.

CHER   A blush with which I'd never paint myself.

JOSH   How, then, shall I help thee unto a groom?

GAIL   [offstage:] O son, my Josh? What, lamb! What, laddie
                                              bird! 45

JOSH   My mother, fie! I fain would hide from her—
        I prithee, Cher, if ever thou wert kind,
        Tell not my mother where I may be found!

        He hides behind an arras. Enter GAIL.

GAIL   O, Cher, 'tis thee. An unexpected joy.
        My son, is he herein? I'd speak with him.   50
        Hath he been cleaning out thine ice house with
        His appetite ne'er-ending?

CHER   —Nay, ex-step,
        He is not here, nor hath been, nor shall be.
        Try thou the dormitory where he liveth—
        Belike he spends the evening studying.   55

GAIL   A scholar from the minute he was born.
        My thanks, Cher, for thy helpfulness.

CHER   —Farewell.
                              [Exit Gail. Josh comes forward.

JOSH   Thou art most gracious and kindhearted, lass—
              Thy quality of mercy is not strain'd.

CHER   Why wouldst thou hide from thine own mother, Josh? 60

JOSH   My school's spring holidays are near enow,
              And she would have me to the nest return.

CHER   But thou wouldst fly the coop. Yet wherefore so?
              No other little chicks shall be in school—
              Why, then, hie not beneath thy mother's wings?   65

JOSH   The rooster—husband number four is he—
              Doth rule the roost. He's foolish as a fowl,
              Believing acting like a family
              Means he may criticize and peck at me
              Whenever and however he desires.   70

CHER   How shalt thou pass the dreary fortnight's span?
              Wilt thou go roaming round the campus by
              Thyself and haunt the buildings as if thou
              Wert spectral and the school thy haunted house?

JOSH   I do not mind the time alone.

CHER   —Hast thou   75
              Lost all thy sense and sensibility?
              Come hither to the house, take thine old room,
              And join thou in the balls that we shall host.

JOSH   Nay, but I thank thee.

CHER   —Wherefore wilt thou not?

JOSH   Thou hast a social galaxy entire—   80
              The planets, moons, and quasars in their courses,
              With thee, the bright sun, at its center point—
              Therein would I be mere impediment.

CHER   Thou couldst ne'er be impediment, in sooth.

JOSH   Wouldst thou want some ex-half-stepbrother type   85
              To orbit round thy dances and soirées?

CHER   Though once our parents were conjoin'd, thou art
              No brother mine.

JOSH   —Yet thou dost know my meaning.

CHER   Have some excitement in thy gloomy life—
              The universe shines brightly when one sees   90
              The stars of all the firmament array'd.
              Thou shalt replenish'd be for thine exams,
              Which even thou—whose head may sometimes be
              As rigid as a meteor—canst see.

JOSH   Thou hast o'erwhelm'd my better sense with this,   95
              Thine otherworldly pow'r of argument.

CHER   'Tis well—such fun we'll have!

JOSH   —How did I come
              Unto the point where I accept advice
              From one who liketh drawings in her books?

CHER   I'll not take heed whilst thou insult'st Sirs Wren   100
              And Stimpious, who are philosophers
              Most existential. For, as it is said,
              Cogito ergo stultus sum, in sooth.

JOSH   The words outpouring from thine untrain'd mouth:
              Hast e'en a jot or tittle of what thou   105
              Art saying?

CHER   —Nay, yet sound as though I do!
              Alas, the heaviness of sleep o'ercomes me,
              And I must to my room. Good night, kind Josh.
                                              [Exit Cher.

JOSH   She hath invited me to spend my school's
              Spring holidays residing in this house.   110
              Although her heart toward her Christian turns,

I cannot be dismay'd at this event—
This sudden warmth in our relationship.
Such I'll not press, but let fate take its time
And see what doth transpire in th'interim.   115
Who knows but that we two may yet be friends?
Bewildering's her attitude to me,
Yet 'tis a wonder I'll bear happily.

[Exit.

ACT IV

SCENE 1

The Horowitz house.

Enter CHER *and* DIONNE.

CHER   My Christian said that he would call on me
        Upon the morrow, which, in boyish time,
        Translates to Thursday. Pray imagine, then,
        My great surprise that he shall come tonight!
        He wishes to deliver merriments—   5
        A newfound form of entertainment, which
        As yet is unbeknownst to me, and that
        The two of us together shall explore.
        A night alone with Christian! This is why
        I've sent for thee, to reinforce my nerves.   10

DIONNE   A lighting concept for thy sitting room
        We must design, to set the mood aright,
        And then decide what garments thou shalt wear—
        A costume fit for catching stylish lads.

CHER   The mirror telleth naught but lies to me—   15
        Pray, render me a portrait I shall see.
                    [Dionne draws Cher in various outfits.

DIONNE   'Tis said that when a lad doth come to call,
        One must have foodstuffs cooking on a spit,
        With fine aromas to ensnare the nose,
        Which shall lead him to thee like fish on hook.   20

CHER   An excellent suggestion, verily—
        I'll put this lump of flesh upon the flames
        And let the fragrance waft to Christian's nostrils.

[They put meat over the fire.
My face, methinks, still hath a reddish hue.

DIONNE   I'll paint thee to appear as white as snow,   25
Yet thou art flush'd, and must unwind thy nerves,
Which yet are tightly coil'd, an 'twere a spring.

CHER   As I bethink upon my maidenhead,
How happy am I that I spent it not
On someone for whom feelings were lukewarm.   30
My Christian is a most attractive man;
This night shall I remember evermore.

DIONNE   Blot now thy lips—thou art as ready as
Thou canst be.

CHER   —Thank you, Dionne, for thy help.
[A bell rings.
Ah! Christian comes, mine evening must begin.   35

DIONNE   This is my cue to exit instantly—
Farewell, sweet Cher, and may thine evening shine!

[Exit Dionne. Cher answers the door.

Enter CHRISTIAN, *bearing picture book*
merriments, playbills, and portraits.

CHRISTIAN   Good even, miss.

CHER   —Holla.

CHRISTIAN   —Doth something burn?

I sense a smoldering within the air,

As if 'twere Mass with extra thuribles.   40

CHER   Alas—the meat!

               [They rush to the kitchen, where the meat is
               burning. Cher quickly removes it from the fire.

CHRISTIAN   —My sweet, thou cook'd for me.

'Tis like we two are married and play house.

CHER   I tried, yet fail'd.

CHRISTIAN   —Show me thine ample home.

            [They begin walking around the house.

Thy father hath well-rounded tastes in art,

And his collection shows variety.   45

CHER   He is no connoisseur of art, yet saith

To purchase artwork is a venture sound.

CHRISTIAN   He is no fool, thy father—quite astute.

This sculpture is Claes Oldenburg, methinks.

CHER   A sculptor of renown and worldwide fame.   50

CHRISTIAN   This other piece is older, canst thou see?

Transitional—a most important piece.

CHER   [*aside:*] Who knew he was so riveted by art?

Would he not rather bed me than display

That he knows ev'ry style of furniture?   55

[*To Christian:*] Shall we do as merfolk are wont to do,

	And take a plunge within my fam'ly's pool?
CHRISTIAN	An occupation far too wet by half—
	Let us inside, to view my merriments.

> *[They go inside and lounge together on a*
> *bed, looking at Christian's picture book*
> *merriments, playbills, and portraits.*

CHER	[*aside:*] Whilst ordinarily this entertainment	60
	Would hold some fascination for me, now
	It seemeth this is only a delay,
	A prelude to the evening's main event.
	These pictures are delightful, in their way,
	Yet I am much distracted presently.	65
	My Christian loves the artist Tony Curtis
	And brought a number of his pictures here:
	Spartronicus and *As Some Like It Hot.*
	I'll let him know of mine intentions with
	A subtle sweeping of my supple foot.	70

> *[She rubs her foot against Christian,*
> *and he moves away uncomfortably.*

CHRISTIAN	Is this a game of footsie thou wouldst play?
CHER	My feet are cold; I hop'd thou wouldst give warmth.
CHRISTIAN	This well-fluff'd pillow, o'er the top of them,
	Shall give thee all the heat thou canst desire.

> *[He places a pillow upon her feet.*

	View what comes next, for 'tis a thrilling part.	75
CHER	[*aside:*] Alas, unto the pages he doth turn,
	As if his picture books were ev'rything!
	I'll make my face the sign of wantonness,
	That he may know here lies a much-inclin'd—

> *[She tries to look alluring and, in doing so,*
> *loses her balance and falls off the bed.*

CHRISTIAN   Art thou well, Cher?

CHER   —In troth, ne'er was I better.   80
             Wouldst thou have aught to drink? Perhaps some wine,
             To lubricate the workings of our night?

CHRISTIAN   Nay—hast thou notic'd wine has the effect
             Of making people emphasize their sex?

CHER   Yet 'tis no bother. 'Tis a glad result,   85
             If thus to emphasize may further lead,
             Attended with the pleasures of the world.

CHRISTIAN   [aside:] Alas, a lass again caught 'neath my spell,
             Though I desire it not nor wish'd it so.
             [To Cher:] My spirit hath grown tir'd, and I must leave. 90

CHER   Some coffee shall revive thy spirit faint!

CHRISTIAN   Mine ulcer shall be writhing if I drink't.

CHER   Yet thou had many cappuccinos once
             And made no mention of an ulcer's pain.

CHRISTIAN   'Tis mostly foam, which—like the seaside's waves,   95
             Which do but stand upon the foaming shore—
             Doth grant one health, detracting not therefrom.

CHER   Wilt thou be gone so soon?

CHRISTIAN   —Pray, hear me, Cher:
             Thou art a wonder. Are we two not friends?

CHER   We are.

CHRISTIAN   —Grant me a kiss upon my cheek.   100
                                 [She kisses his cheek.
             My maiden sweet, farewell.
                                     [Exit Christian.

CHER   —What scene was this?
             Have I some fault—can flat hair blamèd be?
             Did I upon some awkward lighting fall?
             O Christian, if thou couldst but tell me what

I did that hath so disenchanted thee,   105
'Twill be address'd! The problem must be me.

                                                    [Exit.

SCENE 2

The streets of Beverly Hills.

Enter DIONNE *and* MURRAY, *driving in her carriage.*

DIONNE   A message I receiv'd from Cher today,
            Who told me of her disappointing night
            With her perplexing newfound paramour.
            She is confounded by the manner that
            He did display when they had time alone.   5
            I bid thee, hound her not for details, please,
            For she is delicate and vulnerable.

MURRAY   More worried over thy new driving skills
            Am I than over Cher's romantic life.
            Upon the theme of Cher and her new beau,   10
            I shall withhold my tongue and be like one
            Who doth but listen, with no pow'r to speak.

DIONNE   Thou, Murray, art a worthy gentleman.

                    Enter CHER, *climbing into the*
                    carriage with them. They drive on.

CHER   Directly to the point, my caring friends—

	What's wrong with me, that someone would not take 15
	Delight in mine appearance or myself?
DIONNE	Belike the lad was truly tir'd, 'tis all.
CHER	Perhaps the match was not our destiny—
	The lad doth finer garments own than mine.
	What could I bring to such relationship? 20
MURRAY	[*to Dionne:*] Beware of all the lanes—an thou wouldst change,
	What must thou do?
DIONNE	—First, make my signal clear.

[She begins to signal and turns her head aside.]

MURRAY	Nay, watch the road, or thou mayst wreck us.
DIONNE	—Tut!
	Thy shouting shall not calm my weary nerves.
	Next, in my mirror gaze, that I may view 25
	Another carriage coming up behind,
	And check the blind spot, to be wholly safe.

[She turns her head, and the carriage swerves wildly.]

MURRAY	Turn with thy head yet not the carriage whole!
	By heaven, lass, thy driving wretchèd is!
DIONNE	I shall not hear thee, who would silent be. 30
MURRAY	My silence was not promis'd unto thee.
CHER	To be capricious o'er my maidenhood
	Was foolish—glad am I that nothing came.
	Dee, nearly did I give myself to him.
MURRAY	Who is this man, who hath rejected thee? 35
CHER	'Twas Christian, who hath nearly ta'en my sex.

[Murray laughs heartily.]

| DIONNE | So quickly turn'd from listen unto laugh? |
| | What is so humorous? |

MURRAY   —Are ye both blind?
Hath aught affected your collective eyes,
That ye see not the matter, which is clear   40
To anyone who hath the pow'r of sight?
Thy would-be paramour, this Christian, is
Less likely to be lover than be squire,
More likely to taste cake of his own kind,
Less likely to enjoy romantic dancing,   45
More likely to be on the disco floor,
Less likely to be wild than to read Wilde,
More likely to be one of Streisand's lads,
Less like to Dor'thy date than be her friend—
Is not my meaning obvious to thee?   50

CHER   A lad's lad? Nay.

MURRAY   —The lad is gay, forsooth:
He makes his heaven in a fellow's lap,
And decks his body in gay ornaments,
And witches sweet chaps with his words and looks.

CHER   Not even—

MURRAY   —Yea, most even, verily.   55

DIONNE   Thou must admit, Cher, he doth like to shop,
To purchase garments in a vast array.
As thou hast said, the lad is better dress'd
Than many of compeers—e'en ourselves.

CHER   My mind is crawling with these buglike thoughts,   60
Which crawl across my brain an 'twere their nest.
How silly and how reckless I have been!

MURRAY   Fie! Other pressing matters are upon us—
Thou, Dionne, dost approach the boulevard,
Where carriages are far too swift and wild   65
For thy still burgeoning attempts to drive!

	Turn off before disaster doth befall!	
	What hast thou done, thou silly, senseless lass—	
	We all shall die because of thy mistake!	
DIONNE	I cannot stop our progress—we are bound	70
	Unto the boulevard, whatever will!	

They enter a crowded lane, with many carriages
around them. Enter other DRIVERS.

	What shall I do t'escape this misery?	
DRIVER 1	Thou careless girl, where didst thou learn to drive?	
MURRAY	[*to Dionne:*] Alas, we shall be slain upon the road—	
	How careless, fie! Yet I shall guide thee through:	75
	Go forward, rest thy mind and be thou calm.	
	All shall be well, I swear by heaven's name.	
	I here am with thee, and shall ne'er depart,	
	Although thou puttest my life at great risk.	
DRIVER 2	Thou irresponsible and awful wench!	80
MURRAY	Fie, fie upon't that I instructed thee	
	In th'art of city driving—more fool I!	
	Whate'er thou dost, keep hands upon the reins,	
	Lest we shall perish 'midst these hooligans!	
DRIVER 3	I bite my thumb at thee, thou luckless lass!	85
CHER	Alack, alack, we certainly shall die!	
MURRAY	Now to the right, a chance to exit comes.	
	Deliverance, although thou nearly kill'd us!	

                     [*Dionne guides the carriage off the*
                          boulevard. Exeunt other drivers.

DIONNE	We are alive—thou brought me through the storm!	
MURRAY	Sweet life—we still exist, and have not died.	90
	Thou wert a wonder, navigating so!	

I am so proud of thee, my heart may burst.

                        [Dionne begins to cry.

Pray fear no evil, for I am with thee.

Breathe in, breathe out, and let peace wash o'er thee.

      [Dionne and Murray begin kissing passionately.

CHER   [*aside:*] Escaping from the boulevard intact   95

Reminds one how significant love is.

I'll wager Dionne's priz'd virginity

From technical to nonexistent turns

Because of this event. I realize, too,

How much I want a lad to call mine own.   100

[*To Dionne and Murray:*] Farewell, friends, thank you

                        both for new perspective.

                 [Cher climbs from the carriage and exits.

DIONNE   Sweet Murray, where thou art I'll ever be—
           Pray take me homeward, bedward, presently!
MURRAY   My dumpling, Dionne, empress of my heart,
           Where fretfulness doth end, let romance start!   105

                                            [Exeunt.

SCENE 3

Westside Pavilion mall and Bronson Alcott High School.

Enter CHER.

CHER   Good Christian will not be my paramour,
           Yet 'tis a pleasure spending time with him.
           He shall be my new shopping partner, yea,
           And presently he comes to meet me here—
           My place of refuge, Westside Pavilion mall.   5

Enter CHRISTIAN.

CHRISTIAN Good afternoon! Such shopping we shall have.
           Yet where is Tai? Was she not meeting us?
CHER   She met some unknown fellows at a shoppe
           And took them yonder, as thou mayst behold.

Enter TAI *with two* HOOLIGANS. *She sits on a railing over the trap door.*

           These barneys she doth meet—whence come their kind? 10

	She doth attract more refuse than the man	
	Who comes and takes the garbage ev'ry week.	
CHRISTIAN	A question for thee, thou of keenest eye:	
	This doublet that I purchas'd: doth it call	
	To mind James Dean or Jason Priestley, which?	15
	The answer's greater than essential, for	
	One is the paragon of all that's manly,	
	Whilst th'other is a trifling hobbyhorse,	
	The zero found in 90210.	
CHER	Just carpe diem, Christian—thou look'st fine	20
	Array'd in't—let thy misgivings flee!	
CHRISTIAN	Thou art most sure?	
TAI	[to hooligans:] —An I did fall, ye'd catch me?	
HOOL. 1	As surely as I catch a cold in th'rain.	
CHER	Behold their antics—could they be more bland,	
	More unoriginal as they do woo?	25

> [The hooligans grab Tai and hold her over
> the railing, as if threatening to drop her.

TAI	Help! Stop, ye villains! Help! O, bring me up!

> [Christian rushes to give her aid,
> pulling her safely back over the railing
> and out of the hooligans' arms.

CHRISTIAN	You gleeking beetle-headed maggot-pies!
HOOL. 2	'Twas no more than a jest.
CHRISTIAN	—A jest, forsooth!
	You'd play your horrid games with women's lives?

> [Christian pushes them away. Exeunt hooligans.

TAI	Cher, I was sore afeard. I, innocent,	30
	Did sit conversing with the charming lads,	
	When suddenly, amidst the laughter warm,	
	They grabb'd me, pushing me—	

CHRISTIAN	—Tai, art thou well?
TAI	I am.
CHRISTIAN	—Art certain?
TAI	—Verily. My thanks.
	Too much adventure I have had today.
CHRISTIAN	Let's get thee home for needed R and R.
TAI	What do those letters stand for? Ribs and rice?
	[Christian laughs. He and Tai walk on
	together, leaving the mall and walking
	toward school. Cher follows.
CHER	[*aside:*] Considering how clueless young Tai is,
	She plays the part of damsel in distress
	As if she had rehears'd it all her life—
	A perfect actor in her starring role.

35

40

Enter various STUDENTS *at the school, including*
DIONNE *and* AMBER, *sitting down to lunch.* TAI *sits
and begins telling her tale. Exit* CHRISTIAN.

                Observe now how she sitteth round her stage,
                Soliloquizing o'er her incident—
                A harmless jest by mindless hooligans
                Turn'd—like a monologue writ by a bard,   45
                With drama heighten'd—to a brush with death.

STUDENT 2   [*to Tai:*] When thou knock'd on the door of death, what
                                                was
                The vision in your mind? A montage of
                The many scenes thou witness'd in thy life?

TAI   No montage, nay—my brain's not on the A-team—   50
                More like the ending of a tragedy,
                Where all is death before the exeunt omnes.

Enter SUMMER.

SUMMER   Cher, is it true that members of a gang
                Attempted to shoot Tai at yonder mall?

CHER   Nay, though the rumors fly on eagles' wings,   55
                'Tis manifestly, absolutely false.

SUMMER   All do report the news as if 'twere true.

CHER   Whatever you desire to think, you shall—
                E'en when 'tis plainly facts alternative.

STUDENT 2   [*to Tai:*] When I was nine years old, I tumbl'd from 60
                A structure made for play—a gymlike jungle—
                And could have sworn I saw a vision black—
                            [*Cher approaches the group.*

TAI   Make way for Cher, my best and truest friend.

CHER   [*aside:*] Shall she have other folk make way for me?
            My station is revers'd with hers—now am   65
            I supplicant while she is master turn'd.

AMBER   [*to Tai:*] Say more of what befell thee!

TAI   —Where was I?

AMBER   Thou ponder'dst over what is truly vital.

TAI   Of course! Before one dies—as I near did—
            The mind becometh suddenly aware,   70
            As if a fog did clear in one fell swoop.
            'Tis both intense and spiritual as well—

CHER   When I was held at gunpoint recently—

STUDENT 2   [*to Cher:*] Beg pardon, for the lass would tell her tale.
            [*To Tai:*] Go on, I pray. Thy tale, Tai, would cure
                                                    deafness. 75

TAI   It is a matter of the spirit, friends,
            Which I, though, cannot pinpoint for thy mind;
            It is impossible that I discuss
            The subject sans a common frame of ref'rence.

CHER   [*aside:*] Is this some alternate reality,   80
            Wherein I am a meager hanger-on
            And Tai is diva to the yearning masses?
            I'll put my status to the test anon.

TAI   Since ye have ne'er experienc'd the like—

CHER   Tai, to the Tow'r of Records I shall go,   85
            To purchase some small souvenir for Christian.

TAI   Indeed? What is't to me?

CHER   —Wouldst thither come?

TAI   Yea, for I owe the man my very life,
            My health, my whole existence, by my troth.

CHER   Then I shall come for thee when school doth end?   90

TAI   Yet not today, for I have other plans—

	With Amber unto Melrose am I bound.	
AMBER	We two—we best of friends—to Melrose go.	
CHER	Perchance tomorrow better works for thee?	
TAI	Next Monday, peradventure, would suffice.	95
	My week doth fill like bucket 'neath a spout.	
CHER	[*aside:*] I have been snubb'd. Cher Horowitz is snubb'd!	
TAI	[*to Dionne:*] Thy boyfriend hither cometh—ha! A jest—	
	For none in their right mind would choose his kind.	
DIONNE	My Murray? O, I see, 'tis Travis. Ha!	100

Enter TRAVIS.

TRAVIS	Tai, look upon this trick I've master'd.	

> [*He spits a bite of food into the air,*
> *then catches it in his mouth.*

TAI	Disgusting!	
TRAVIS	[*to Dionne:*] —May I sit by Tai's side?	
DIONNE	Nay.	
TAI	—Be thou gone! Do not ye slackers lounge	
	On yonder grassy knoll in infamy?	
TRAVIS	[*aside:*] The lass is changèd, not for better.	105
	She doth abuse me to win favor.	

> [*Exit Travis.*

CHER	[*aside:*] Ne'er felt I sympathy for Travis ere,	
	Yet Tai's mistreatment is deplorable.	
	Is this what I have help'd her to become?	
	Is't possible I so coldhearted am?	110
DIONNE	Tai, let us speak as two mature adults,	
	Who know the ways of pleasure and men's bodies.	
	Hast thou e'er, in the water, done the deed?	
TAI	Yea, natur'lly!	

DIONNE   —E'en so? How does it work?

          [Exeunt all but Cher as she
             wanders off by herself.

CHER   *[aside:]* What is this strange, unlikely circumstance   115
    Where Dionne asketh Tai for love advice
    And Tai exceeds my popularity?
    Hath all the world gone hurly-burly now?
    'Tis like a universe in parallel,
    Where all is similar, yet deeply chang'd.   120
    To make these matters worse, I soon must take
    My driving test, that I may legally
    Direct a carriage on its forward course.
    I shall unto my home, to find my most
    Responsible-appearing outfit. O—   125
    I cannot bear these ripples in my fate,
    Which shall my happy spirit obfuscate.

               [Exit.

SCENE 4

The Horowitz house and the streets of Beverly Hills.

Enter LUCY.

LUCY   How, sometimes, I miss my El Salvador,
    Land whence I came, where I was born and rais'd.
    The child of two adoring parents I,
    Who wish'd a better, broader life for me.

"Stay not within thy native country, Lucy!"   5
So often they directed me, in hopes
That more adventures elsewhere did await.
At twenty-one, unto America
I came with hope and wonder burgeoning,
Sure—in the land of opportunity—   10
My life would flourish with prosperity.
Instead, it seem'd that, as an immigrant—
One for whom Spanish was the native tongue—
I was unwanted, lesser, and the aim
Of ev'ry prejudice some people had.   15
'Twas not prosperity that I did find,
'Twas not adventure that did greet me here.
Instead, I was expected to want less,
Became a cleaner in a rich man's house,
And here I dwell—a woman sans a home.   20

Enter CHER.

CHER	O, Lucy, thou art heaven-sent! Where is
	My shirt sans collar made by Fred'rick Segal?
LUCY	Belike 'tis at the cleaners, Lady Cher.
CHER	Today, though, is my carriage driving test.
	Dost thou not see? The garment makes me look 25
	More capable than any other doth.
LUCY	Shall I call on them for thee?
CHER	—'Tis too late!
	We also—almost I forgot—receiv'd
	Another notice from the fire brigade
	Declaring we must clear the flamm'ble bush. 30
	Didst thou not say José would clip the hedge?

LUCY   He is thy gardener—ask him thyself.

                    Enter JOSH.

CHER   Thou, Lucy, know'st I speak not Mexican.
LUCY   No Mexican am I!
                                        [Exit Lucy, angrily.
CHER   —Why shouted she?
JOSH   Thy Lucy cometh from El Salvador.   35
CHER   Thy point is what?
JOSH   —It is another land,
             A country in its own right, which hath naught
             To do with Mexico.
CHER   —What doth that matter?
JOSH   Thou say'st it matters if someone declares
             Thy house is somewhere south of Sunset, Cher!   40
CHER   Wilt thou not salve my mind? Is't all my fault?
             I am forever wrong, a country girl
             Declaring ever matters incorrect.
JOSH   Thou art a brat—a silly, foolish lass.
                                             [Exit Josh.
CHER   Hath all the world against me harshly turn'd?   45
             First Tai and Dionne, Lucy and then Josh,
             Is no one left who loveth gloomy Cher?

                    Enter DRIVING INSTRUCTOR.

INSTRUCT.   If thou art ready, we'll begin thy test.
CHER   [*aside:*] 'Twas not the comfort for which I did seek.
                             [Cher and the instructor climb into a
                                carriage together, with Cher driving.

An overwhelming ickiness comes o'er me,   50
As waves wash over feet that stand on shore.
I shall apologize to Lucy soon
Enow, yet still my heart is plagu'd with doubt.
For Josh to think me cruel drives me mad,
And makes my driving equally as poor.   55

Enter other DRIVERS *and* PEDESTRIANS *in the lane.*

INSTRUCT.   Move thou into the right lane presently.
CHER   [*aside:*] Why should my mind be troubl'd over the
             Opinion Josh hath of me anywise?
             Why am I into turmoil toss'd to think
             That in his eyes I may have dropp'd a peg?   60
                          [*She veers quickly into the next lane,*
                                almost hitting a pedestrian.

INSTRUCT.   Behold where thou dost turn, or thou shalt kill!
             Wouldst make this carriage be thy murder weapon?
CHER   Alas, 'twas my fault wholly.
INSTRUCT.   —What is this?
             This pretense unto driving doth not make
             Thee yet a driver—thou art not allow'd   65
             To take both lanes, as if thou wert King Henry
             And these two lanes were France and England both.
             As I declar'd before, pull thou into
             The lane upon the right, and do so now.
                          [*Cher pulls into the lane, but in doing*
                                so strikes a parked carriage.
             Nay, not so quickly! Wouldst thou slay us both? 70
             Thou dost more damage than a hurricane!
CHER   Should I leave them a note, to say 'twas me?

INSTRUCT.   Pull over here; the carriage stop anon.

> *[Cher stops the carriage at the side of the*
> *lane. Exeunt other drivers and pedestrians.*

CHER   Shall we drive elsewhere, that thou mayst observe
             How skill'd I am at making left-hand turns?   75

INSTRUCT.   We shall return unto thy house at once—
             My hands grasp'd firmly on the reins, not thine.

> *[He takes the reins and begins driving*
> *the back to Cher's house.*

CHER   The test is over?

INSTRUCT.   —Thankfully, 'tis so.

CHER   Did I, then, pass th'examination, sir?

INSTRUCT.   Consult we two the notes that I have made—   80
             Thou shalt know whether thou hast made the grade.
             Point one: thou art a failure at the art
             Of parking carriages upon the road.
             Point two: thou causest great catastrophes
             When thou attempt'st to switch betwixt two lanes.   85
             Point three: thou art a threat to humankind
             When thou dost try to make a right-hand turn.
             Point four: thou damag'st private property
             As thou dull-wittedly dost drive along.
             Point five: thou nearly kill'd a human soul   90
             By striking them withal thy vehicle.
             Concluding point: were I a betting man,
             I'd venture thou hast fail'd th'examination.

CHER   Ha, failure? Nay, be merciful, say "death."
             For failure hath more terror in his look,   95
             Much more than death; do not say I have fail'd!
             O, may we not begin again, I pray—
             A problem personal doth plague my soul,

Which causeth me to drive with care too short.
Thou saw'st how the pedestrian appear'd   100
As though they had been conjur'd from the air—
A rabbit pull'd from a magician's hat!
Grant me another chance, and thou shalt see
That I shall concentrate most ardently.
In general, I am a driver skill'd!   105
Is there not someone else to whom I may
Converse, complain, convince, and make my case—
Thy supervisor, mayhap? For thou canst
Not be the be-all and the end-all in
The issuing of driver's licenses!   110

INSTRUCT.   As far as thou concernèd are, rash girl,
I am Messiah of all licensing,
The lord and savior of the driving world,
The alpha and omega of thy chances.

                              [They arrive at Cher's house.
Pray, disembark. Thou shalt not drive today.   115
                    *[Cher gets out of the carriage and walks
                        into her house. Exit instructor.*

CHER   It beggars all belief that I did fail!
Ne'er have I met a failure that I could
Not argue my way therefrom. Is this how
Most ordinary human beings feel?

Enter TAI *and* JOSH, *playing a game together.* TAI *holds a box.*

TAI   Holla, thou art return'd!
JOSH   —Cher, welcome home—   120
Apologies for how we parted ways.
How doth it feel to have thy driver's license?

CHER   Those fine sensations I cannot describe;
            I fail'd my test.

TAI   —O Cher, my sympathy.

CHER   Josh, spare me all thy lecturing profound   125
            Upon the subject of the art of driving—
            How 'tis a vast responsibility
            At which, by feigning, one shall not succeed.

JOSH   Thou drivest ev'ry thought thereof from me—
            Those words are thine, not mine.

CHER   —Thy thoughts speak
                                        loud 130
            Enow that I may clearly hear the words.

TAI   Cher, let us talk awhile, for I have aught
            That I would show thee, which may change thy mien.

JOSH   'Tis my cue, then, to bid you both farewell.

            [Exit Josh. Cher and Tai sit next to the fireplace.

TAI   I am most sorry, hearing of thy test,   135
            Yet am so glad thou hast, at length, arriv'd.
            There is a deed that doth fulfillment need,
            But I'd not undertake it sans thine aid.
            Canst sparkle still the right Promethean fire?

CHER   Indeed. One moment, and we shall have flames.   140

                                    [Cher lights the fire.

            The box thou carriest—what is therein?

TAI   'Tis some few trifles that bring Elton to
            My mind, and we two—like Pandora—shall
            Discover ev'ry evil held within.
            Unlike the lass of old, though, we'll not set   145
            Them free upon the world, but burn them in
            The pyre and so release me of their woes.
            My heart hath mov'd beyond him, I am sure.

CHER   Let it be open'd!

TAI   —Dost thy mind recall
              The party in the Valley, where a shoe   150
              Did strike upon my pate and knock me cold?
              Kind Elton brought a tow'l with ice to help.

CHER   [*aside:*] 'Twas Travis who brought ice, as I recall.

TAI   I was embarrass'd, at the time, to tell,
              But I brought home the tow'l as souvenir.   155
                         [*Tai pulls the towel from the box
                              and throws it on the fire.*

CHER   Thou art in jest! A towel?

TAI   —Even so!
              Remember thou the song that play'd whilst we
              Were dancing happily together, he
              And I—'twas that "roll with the homies" song?

CHER   A tune forgettable, and I'd forgot.   160

TAI   In sentiment, I did the music buy,
              And play'd it over nearly ev'ry night.

CHER   Tai, I am happy for thee. Tell me, what
              Brought on this swelling of empowerment?

TAI   I met a man whose character amazeth,   165
              Who makes rank Elton seem most loserly.

CHER   News wonderful!

TAI   —Wilt thou help me win Josh?

CHER   To win Josh what? Thou wouldst win him a prize?

TAI   My meaning is as plain as my delight—
              I like him; gladly would I be with him.   170

CHER   Think'st thou his disposition's mutual?

TAI   Yea, I do spy some marks of love in him.

CHER   What signs or signals hath he given thee?

TAI   The littlest items speak with loudest voice:

	He findeth ways to touch or tickle me.	175
	Recall when we were, lately, at the fest,	
	And I felt lost, forsaken, and depress'd—	
	He rescu'd me by asking me to dance,	
	And whilst we danc'd he flirted like a child.	
	Thy face, though, looketh pale—say, art thou well?	180
CHER	I shall be. [*Aside:*] Nay, I cannot tell the truth.	
	[*To Tai:*] Two mochaccinos did I have, which was	
	At least one drink too many—I may burst!	
TAI	The feeling is precisely known to me—	
	The other day, as I convers'd with Josh,	185
	We did discuss the difference betwixt	
	The girls of high school versus college girls.	
	The girls of college paint their faces less,	
	Which is why lads prefer them over us—	
CHER	Tai, dost thou think that Josh and thou will work?	190
	Is it a pairing made for tales of love?	
	He is a bookworm, nerdy in the height.	
TAI	Have I a head of air, and nothing more?	
	Dost think me challeng'd mentally?	
CHER	—Nay, no!	
	Those words are thine, not mine.	
TAI	—Then, dost thou mean	195
	My status is not high enow for Josh?	
CHER	You two shall not mesh well together, Tai—	
	'Tis like the one is oil, the other water.	
TAI	Thou dost believe we never shall mesh well?	
	Why do I listen to thee anywise?	200
	A virgin with no driver's license, thou.	
CHER	'Tis wondrous harsh, past all necessity.	
TAI	Apologies that I struck thee so low.	

Let us attempt another parley once
Our strong emotions mellow for a spell.   205
Time heals all wounds, so doth the saying go.
Until that moment, I bid thee adieu.

                                        [*Exit Tai.*

CHER   What have I done to my relationships?
         Tai is a monster of mine own design,
         A Gorgon with a steely-ey'd resolve.   210
         My gorge is rising, mighty chunks therein,
         That I shall vomit if I get not air—
         I must outside, and rest myself awhile.

                    [*She walks outside, through the streets.*

         All that I think and do is proven wrong!
         Wrong over Elton and his purposes,   215
         Wrong over Christian and what he desires,
         Wrong over Josh and how I should treat him.
         To one conclusion doth the kettle boil,
         Which bubbles over with its meaning plain:
         I am a clueless lass, and nothing more!   220
         The Josh and Tai romance, if it be so,
         Hath overwrought my mind enormously.
         Why should I be concern'd? Tai is my friend!
         I never shall begrudge her happiness—
         If she has suitors, should I not be glad?   225
         Why hath she, though, besotted been with Josh?
         He dresseth like a jester wanting laughs,
         He listeneth to music horrible,
         He is not even cute, convention'lly.
         He is more slug than man, who hangs around   230
         The house and bothers me with teasing jibes.
         How I recall our scenes domestic, he

With mouth stuff'd full of savory delights.
He hath no sense of rhythm, cannot dance—
In sooth, I could not take him anywhere.   235
Before mine eyes I see him at the party,
As he did jump around with bunny hops.
Yet, wherefore do I stress about him so?
This is but Josh. Indeed, he is a Baldwin—
With Alec's gentle smile and lovely hair,   240
And William's youthfulness and sense of style,
With Stephen's frame and utter goofiness,
And Daniel's reticence and striking eyes.
My heart hath memoriz'd his lovely smile,
Like light that brightens up the darkest room.   245
What joy, though, would he find in Tai's embrace?
What could he see in her, a simple girl,
He who is older, more intelligent.
Mayhap he hath the sculptor's eye, which sees
Not lump of rock but beauty just beneath,   250
And then by skill reveals a work of art.
Methinks she would not make him happy long—
Josh needeth someone with imagination,
A person who can render him the care
He needs, for in some areas he's weak,   255
E'en someone who will laugh at all his jests,
Though some deserve but little merriment.
A-ha! The truth is on me suddenly—

*[The fountain behind Cher suddenly
springs forth with water and light.*

Eureka, I have fall'n in love with Josh!
Josh, he whom I have known since I was small,   260
Who tickles me and jabs me when nearby,

Who gives me cause to smile when I am sad,
Whose presence is a comfort in itself,
Who help'd me learn to drive my carriage well,
Whom I do dearly love to torment so,   265
Who, all these years, hath been a friend to me—
By heaven, it is he I love, none other!
Completely, totally, and majorly
My heart doth move toward him utterly!

                                        [Exit.

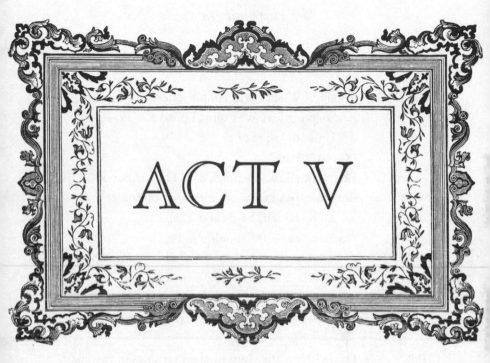

ACT V

SCENE 1

The Horowitz house.

Enter BALTHASAR *on balcony.*

BALTHASAR   [*singing:*] When I was younger, needed I no one
              And making love was sport I plied for fun—
                  Those days are gone,
                  I live alone.
              I think of all the friends whom I have known   5
              But when I call on them they are not home,
                  All by myself, I would not be
                  All by myself, I should not be.

                                        [Exit Balthasar.

Enter CHER *and* JOSH. *They sit together, reading sections
of a newspaper, but she appears bewildered and rigid.*

CHER   [*aside:*] Now that I know the yearnings of my heart,
              How shall I act when I am near my Josh?   10
              In ordinary circumstances, I
              Would strut, like pretty-plumèd peacock—by
              His side, array'd in garments au courant,
              Would send myself bouquets or chocolates,
              Yet how can I ply petty games with Josh?   15
JOSH   What is the matter, Cher?
CHER   —What meanest thou?
JOSH   Thy wont is to be noisier than this—
              Thou art as silent as a mouse in church.

Here we have sat awhile, yet thou hast not
Discuss'd the *Real World* goings-on as yet. 　　20

CHER The real world doth present itself in news—
Reports of all the sadness of the globe,
Which I attend with open, eager ears.

JOSH This is a change—news ne'er did int'rest thee,
Or such thou ever didst report to me. 　　25

CHER Now have I chang'd.

JOSH 　　　　　　　　—Yet thou dost look confus'd.

CHER Methought they had declar'd a final peace
For all who dwell within the Middle East,
Yet these reports describe more skirmishes
Among the peoples of those nations proud. 　　30

JOSH [*aside:*] Was e'er a silly mind so beautiful,
So simple, and so open unto hope?
[*To Cher:*] I must to class. 'Til later, au revoir.

　　　　　　　　[*Exit Josh. Cher begins pacing in
　　　　　　　　front of her father's office.*

　　　　　　Enter MEL HOROWITZ.

MEL Cher, come thou hither.

　　　　　　　　　　　　[*Cher goes to him.*

CHER 　　　　　　—Father, what is it?

MEL Unless thou hast into a vulture turn'd— 　　35
Which paceth to and fro and back and forth
Until a living animal hath turn'd
To carrion that sates the appetite—
Thou shouldst not tut about like one who waits.
Hast thou some matter burning in thy heart 　　40
That causeth thee to fret and sigh and groan?

	Why dost thou dance athwart my office door	
	As if thou had some issue to discuss	
	Yet wert afraid to bring the matter forth?	
CHER	Naught, nay, not I. Mere help I'd proffer thee,	45
	If thou hadst any task for mine employ.	
MEL	A gracious and most admirable lass—	
	Thou canst give aid, if thou art willing. See,	
	Here is a deposition for review.	
	Look carefully upon the records here—	50
	Each time thou comest on a dialogue	
	That happen'd on September third last year,	
	Take thou the quill and make thy mark beside,	
	That later we may spot it easily.	
	September third—no other date but this.	55
CHER	I understand and shall fulfill the task.	

[Cher takes the papers and the
quill and begins working.

MEL	[*aside:*] To have my daughter working by my side—	
	Was ever father fortunate as I?	
	In all my visions of a future time,	
	Ne'er did I dare to hope it would be thus.	60
	[*To Cher:*] 'Tis somewhat fun, is't not?	
CHER	—I would not call	
	My friends together for a game like this,	
	Yet 'tis a task agreeable enow.	
	May I ask, Father: didst thou ever have	
	A problem that thou couldst not argue thy	65
	Way therefrom? Hast thou ever met with such?	
MEL	[*aside:*] My guileless daughter is as plain to read	
	As volumes set in letters printed large—	
	I knew there was some matter on her heart.	

	[*To Cher:*] Tell me the problem and, together, we	70
	Shall figure out the argument it needs.	
CHER	There is a lad—	
MEL	[*aside:*] —There ever is, in troth!	
CHER	Yet he hath set his heart on someone else.	
MEL	How could that be? Thou art Cher Horowitz!	
	Thy popularity hath e'er excell'd,	75
	Thy powers of persuasion are renown'd,	
	Thy witticisms are unmatchable,	
	Thy splendor known to all who look on thee.	
CHER	I know not, Father, yet I wretched feel—	
	Rejected by the man I so admire.	80
	I am accustom'd to the highest place,	
	Yet must accept I merely am next best—	
	An unpick'd choice within a narrow field,	
	A second-place contestant in a race,	
	An also-ran unto a better mare.	85
MEL	This errant boy, whoever he may be—	
	Whatever parents poorly brought him up—	
	Moronic is, and guilty of a crime	
	Against humanity: neglecting thee.	
	In all the Hills of Beverly, there is	90
	No lass whose beauty—inside, outside both—	
	Surpasseth thine. Thou art th'epitome	
	Of what a modern woman hopes to be.	
	I shall speak plainly: 'tis my ardent hope	
	Thou shalt not waste thy time with such a one	95
	Who is so blind, so foolish, and so cruel.	
CHER	The truth is, he is most intelligent—	
	A scholar, stuff'd with knowledge and keen sense.	
	He is the type of person to do good,	

	To think of others in their lowly state	100
	And seek how they may gain equality.	
	Mine own activities seem far too small—	
	The after-school commitments I fulfill,	
	Compar'd to him, still are not good enow.	
MEL	How canst thou say this? Or, indeed, e'en think't?	105
	Who taketh care of ev'ryone herein?	
	Who watches over all within our house?	
	Who doth insist her father eateth well?	
	Cher, verily, I've not seen such good done	
	Since thy sweet mother, whom I love, hath died.	110
CHER	O, Father, truly?	
MEL	—I'd not lie to thee—	
	Thy spirit is too honest for deceit.	
	Though I may ply duplicity in court,	
	Thou art the judge to whom I'll swear to tell	
	The truth, the whole truth, nothing but the truth.	115
	Now, to thy work, thou sweet and precious lamb.	
	Thou ne'er shall know how fortunate I am.	

[Exeunt.

SCENE 2

*Bronson Alcott High School, the
Horowitz house, and the park.*

Enter LADY TOBY GEIST.

GEIST   O misery, what I have learn'd today—
Our friends in Pismo Beach, which is a town
Not far from where we live, have been beset
By a disaster worse than can be nam'd!
A rare southwester wind hath ravag'd them   5
With hurricane that left the coastal town
So flooded that the people living there
Have lost near ev'rything. By heav'n above,
Why were the gods so angry at this hamlet?
They say the monarch butterflies are gone,   10
Which migrate ev'ry year to Pismo Beach—
The butterflies, the butterflies, alack!
Shall not e'en butterflies be spar'd this wrath?
My class arriveth any moment—I
Must strong be, and will draw them, if I may,   15
Into a project to save Pismo Beach,
Where I have spent so many happy days
And tasted all the clams that I can eat.

      Enter CHER, DIONNE, TAI, ELTON, *and other*
        STUDENTS, *sitting down for class.*

    Come, students, feel the ardor of my speech,
And let your hearts incline to Pismo Beach!   20
CHER   [*aside:*] The Pismo Beach disaster is the theme
That I, in class, should think upon today,
Yet on my mind is something else entirely—
I need a makeover profound, complete,
But this time 'tis my soul to be made o'er.   25
What makes someone a better person, though?
Is it some designation from on high,

Divine announcement of a person's good?
My friends are good in manners myriad:
Kind Christian wants whatever he observes   30
To be both beautiful and interesting.
When Dionne and her Murray think that none
Are watching them, they are considerate
Of one another's thoughts and points of view,
As one would never know who saw them sparring.   35
Poor Lady Geist—she cries at tragedies,
Which strike her very center with their weight.
E'er doth she strive to win our lazy hearts—
Get us involv'd in causes virtuous—
No matter how intensely we resist.   40

GEIST   What we have read within the news today
Cannot begin to tell the horrid tale—
Each mem'ry, each possession that you have,
Imagine if 'twere stripp'd away at once,
Gone with the wind, and no one gives a damn.   45
Can ye imagine how such things must feel?

                              [Elton raises his hand.

Yea, Elton, thou opinion hast thereon?
ELTON   Pray, Lady Geist, may I use our hall pass?
GEIST   Thou mayst. Class, we shall soon collect some goods,
Which may be sent to folk in Pismo Beach   50
To help them to their swift recovery:
Warm blankets, swaddling clothes for newborn babes,
Nonperishable foodstuffs.
CHER   —Lady Geist?
GEIST   What is it, Cher?
CHER   —I fain would help thy cause.
GEIST   [*aside:*] Surprising and most gracious offer, this!   55

            [*To Cher:*] 'Twould be delightful—gladly I accept!
                    [The bell rings. Exeunt all except Cher,
                             who walks home.

CHER   Already doth a weight lift from my soul!
            The people poor and pain'd of Pismo Beach
            Shall meet another force of nature: Cher.

      She enters the house. Enter MEL HOROWITZ, JOSH,
          and many CLERKS *working together.*

            Sweet father, I am home to gather food   60
            To help the denizens of Pismo Beach;
            Remember the red caviar thou bought'st?
            Thou didst not like it, would not more consume?
MEL   What is she doing?
JOSH   —She's thy daughter, Mel.
            If thou know'st not, I too am clueless, sir.   65
                  [Cher goes to her room and begins
                     looking through her wardrobe.

CHER   [*aside:*] My clothing, too! Of mine abundance I
            Shall happily and generously give—
            So many items out of fashion are
            That I may part with them most painlessly.
                [She gathers clothing in bags and carries them to
                 the front of the house, past her father, Josh, and
                 the lawyers. She gathers skis and tennis rackets.
MEL   What art thou doing, Cher? Thou flit'st about   70
            Like mother bird constructing her new nest.
            Canst thou give me compelling reason for
            The hustle and the bustle thou art at?
CHER   'Tis beating in my mind—I'm captain of

	The Pismo Beach Disaster Aid Brigade.	75
MEL	Methinks they shall not need thy cast-off skis.	
CHER	Some people lost their every possession—	
	Think'st thou their losses do not reach unto	
	Equipment for athletics, Father, eh?	
MEL	Josh, speak: is this thine influence at work?	80
JOSH	Who knows or can recount the ways of Cher?	

> *[Exeunt Mel and lawyers. Cher begins*
> *walking back to school carrying all*
> *of the goods she has collected.*

[Aside:] Cher labors strenuously at this task—
Behemoth in proportion to the tasks
She undertaketh in her daily toil.
Already hath she gather'd many bags   85
Of household items for her enterprise.
'Tis like she'd slay Leviathan to serve
A people she ne'er hath nor ne'er will meet.
How telling of the lady's character.

> *[Exit Josh. Cher returns to school.*

CHER	Come, citizens of Bronson Alcott High,	90
	And join me in a generous crusade!	
	The weary folk in Pismo Beach—beset	
	By danger and disaster all around—	
	Shall know that we, in Hills of Beverly,	
	Have heard their cries resounding in our ears,	95
	Such that our caring hearts were movèd to	
	Respond unto their plight immediately!	

Enter MURRAY, DIONNE, TAI, ELTON, AMBER, *and other* STUDENTS
bearing various goods, raising banners about the Pismo Beach disaster,
and gathering donations into boxes. Enter BALTHASAR *on balcony.*

BALTHASAR   [*singing:*] Shake ye the ground, 'tis action that I need!

            Such shall let me burst forth at utmost speed.

            Be certain, this is all ye e'er shall need   100

              To live the higher meaning of your creed.

                           [*Exit Balthasar.*

CHER   [*to student:*] Canst take these pieces thou hast hither

                                     brought

            And place them with the bedding items yon?

            My gratitude, that thou deliver'd them.

                Enter LADY TOBY GEIST.

            O, Lady Geist, I need more boxes, ma'am.   105

            These we were given nearly are fill'd up.

GEIST   So soon? What noble work thy team hath done!

CHER   The boxes are divided into halves:

            One box for appetizers, one for entrées—

            Though people may be hungry, they must eat   110

            With the sophistication that's their wont.

GEIST   Er . . . yes. Well done—I shall have these ta'en hence.

              Enter TRAVIS, *bearing boxes.*

TRAVIS   Holla, Cher, I have brought donations.

CHER   My thanks! 'Tis decent, Travis, in the height.

                     [*She looks through the boxes*

                           and pulls out a pipe.

            Thou brought'st this implement for folks' relief?   115

TRAVIS   By Jove, I did not know if 'twas right.

            Of it I've no need anymore, yet

            Nor would I e'er deny another

Great pleasures therefrom if they want them.

CHER   Undoubtedly someone will love to have't!   120

TRAVIS   Another word I must deliver:
         I owe thee mine apologies for
         Thy shoes I damag'd at the party.

CHER   Which shoes were those?

TRAVIS   —Red ones with strap things.

CHER   No bother, they were from last season born,   125
         And fall behind what is in fashion now.
         What made thee think on them, that thou felt mov'd
         Most needlessly to render thy regrets?

TRAVIS   'Tis one of my new steps. My new club—
         It hath these steps, a certain number . . .   130

CHER   Twelve steps?

TRAVIS   —Indeed! How knewest thou, Cher?
         Twelve like the astrological signs,
         Twelve like the group of first apostles,
         Twelve like the extra Seahawks teammate,
         Twelve like the angry men in stories.   135

CHER   'Twas just my guess.

TRAVIS   —A guess most wondrous!
         One final thing: take thou this flyer.

                              [He hands her a somewhat
                                 crumpled piece of paper.

CHER   What do these letters ASL denote?

TRAVIS   The Amateur Skateboarding League, sooth.
         The clarity I've found has brought me   140
         Unto a whole new skating level—
         Thou must behold it. Wilt thou join me
         On Saturday, my deeds to witness?

CHER   I shall. [*Aside:*] How good it feels to bring him joy!

TRAVIS   'Tis wonderful. Until the weekend!   145
CHER   And for this pipe—take it to kitchenware?
TRAVIS   Well thought! 'Tis where I us'd to keep it.

                                        [Exeunt all but Cher.

CHER   The next days pass'd, delighted and content.
              My heart, with my newfound activities,
              Began to lift. 'Tis certain giving back   150
              And helping others in their time of need
              Doth wonders for the egocentric soul.
              How sweet of Travis to look past my wrongs,
              The ways that I have him slander'd him before,
              And find the grace t'invite me to his show.   155
              With eagerness I look'd to Saturday—
              Where once I might have scoff'd at Travis and
              Been mortified to see his skateboard act,
              Now I look forward to the great event.

Enter TRAVIS *among other* SKATERS *and the* AUDIENCE *at the
skateboard exhibition. An* ANNOUNCER *introduces* SKATERS
as they perform to cheers. Enter TAI, *approaching* CHER.

TAI   Cher, may we speak? My heart is burning, friend.   160
CHER   Of course.
TAI   —In agony my soul has dwelt
              This past week whole. Yea, I cannot believe
              The angry and excessive words I us'd,
              Which set a barrier twixt thee and me.
CHER   'Tis I descend a spiral built of shame!   165
              How unsupportive and unkind I was,
              That I could not hear of thy love for Josh.
TAI   Thou art entitl'd to thine own opinion—

	'Twas I who did thee wrong, not thou to me.
	From our first meeting, thou wert ever kind—	170
	Forsooth, Cher, hear my words: I would not wish
	Any companion in the world but thee.
CHER	Still, if 'twere not for my o'eractive mind—
	My vain endeavors to create a match—
	Thou never wouldst for Elton spar'd a thought.	175
	Apologies, Tai.
TAI	—I am sorry, Cher!
	Now shall I weep, with tears of happiness.
CHER	Let us make solemn vows to never fight.

[They embrace.

ANNOUNC.	The skater next upon our merry ramp
	Is Travis Birkenstock. Pray wish him well,	180
	That our half-pipe be wholly his today!
CHER	[*to Tai:*] 'Tis Travis! Let us sit and watch him skate!

[They sit. Travis skates majestically.

	[*Aside:*] How easy 'tis, another to dismiss—
	As I observ'd him making jests in class,
	Appearing dimmer than a nighttime shadow,	185
	Ne'er had I guess'd he had such art within.
TAI	Hurrah for Travis!
CHER	—I had no idea
	He was so motivated by this sport.
TAI	Such have I known for months, 'tis clear in him!
CHER	[*aside:*] Behold the sparks the sizzle through the air	190
	Twixt Tai and Travis, two true treasures they!
	Their love is like a fire that's set to blaze.
	I see it in her eye—no thought of Josh
	Remaineth in her steady, fervent gaze.
	They shall be join'd as one, a romance pure—	195

Their hearts in passion amorous entwin'd,
Despite the meddling I had once design'd.

[Exeunt.

SCENE 3

The Horowitz house.

Enter JOSH *and a* CLERK, *working.*

JOSH   [*aside:*] This case is tedious past ev'ry measure,
Yet hath a trifold purpose, verily:
To render some assistance unto Mel,
To grow mine understanding of the law,
And to keep me within the house, near Cher.   5

Enter CHER, *with her hair in braids.*

CHER   How goes the work? I'll help thee, if thou wish'st.
JOSH   My wish is thine, an thou wilt help me work.
                         [*She sits next to him. They grin
                                and glance at each other.*
Thy hair hath the appearance of a girl's—
Is Pippi Longstocking thy paragon?
CHER   That hat gives thee the mien of Forrest Gump.   10
I prithee, who is Pippi Longstocking?
                 [*Cher unbinds her braid and shakes out
                    her hair, while Josh watches her fondly.*

JOSH   A part Mel Gibson never hath portray'd.

CHER   Thou art turn'd jester.

CLERK   [*aside:*]   —I may vomit yet—
         These two flirt like two cottontails in heat.
         [*To Josh:*] What happen'd to the files that were just
                                                    here, 15
         For August twenty-eighth?

JOSH   —Beg pardon, what?

CLERK   Mel wanted them tonight, and there were once
         Full double the amount that sit here now.
         He shall erupt in anger—where are they?

CHER   Alas, methinks I check'd their content for   20
         The conversations of September third.

CLERK   E'en so?

JOSH   —Where didst thou put them, Cher?

CHER   —Two piles
         Created I, dividing them in twain.
         Was't incorrect?

CLERK   —We must redo it wholly!
         Art thou an idiot, thou fawning lout?   25

JOSH   She did not know—I bid thee watch thy words.
         I'll not have thee abuse her cruelly.

CLERK   She set us back another day or more!
         When no one looks for the September call,
         She spends her time thereon! We are undone!   30

CHER   Apologies.

CLERK   —Forget what thou hast done
         And take thine empty head unto the mall.
                                   [*Cher walks aside, crying.*

JOSH   [*to clerk:*] What is thy problem, clack dish? Wherefore
                                                          be
              Ye so unkind unto this harmless lass?
CLERK   I shall be fir'd since she moronic is.   35
JOSH   She is no moron. If thou sett'st thy mind
              Upon what thou hadst been assign'd, 'twould not
              Have happen'd—say thou moron only if
              Thou shalt look in the mirror and so speak.
CLERK   If thou wert working 'stead of wooing, she   40
              Would not be such a bother hereabout.
                              [*The clerk packs up his things to leave.*
JOSH   What baseless accusation's this, thou rogue?
CLERK   Thou knowest what I mean precisely, Josh—
              This is a multimillion ducat case,
              Not thine excuse to play at puppy love.   45
JOSH   We have work'd steadily upon this suit,
              With steadfast purpose and unflagging toil.
CLERK   Now thou and she may toil howe'er ye shall
              And work upon your purpose of romance—
              For my part, I shall sickness claim today.   50
                              [*Exit clerk. Josh approaches
                                Cher and sits next to her.*
CHER   Is't true I have destroy'd the lawsuit whole?
JOSH   Nay, for destruction thou art suited not.
CHER   Did I, then, set him back beyond all hope?
              So much work still remaineth to be done,
              And he can ill afford to lose this time.   55
JOSH   Put all thy hopes on me, thy loser friend,
              For through my care the work may yet be done.

The matter shall not make his spirit ill;
No time or labor shall be lost, I swear.
Canst thou imagine what the blackguard spake?   60
To make thee worry needlessly, as he
Did, was an action most detestable.
'Twas his fault that the work was not fulfill'd,
Yet he would blame us for flirtatiousness.
Imagine saying we were—well, thou know'st.   65

CHER   Thou knowest well, and have devoted been
Unto this case—no fault or blame could e'er
Fall on thy shoulders, thou who labor'st so.

JOSH   The case hath been an opportunity
For me to learn more of the law's delays,   70
The insolence of office and the spurns
That patient merit of th'unworthy takes.
For I, who one day hopes to lawyer be,
'Twas an experience profound and useful.
Thou, though, hath not a need to labor thus.   75
Go out and spend thy days in carefree joy—
Unto the mall fly with thy merry friends
And gather thee thy rosebuds whilst thou may.

CHER   Belike thou think'st 'tis all I ever do,
To pass my days in joyful merriment—   80
Experienc'd in spending, nothing more,
A harpy with her father's ducats arm'd.

JOSH   Nay, prithee, 'twas not mine intent at all.
Thou—er. I . . . um. We—ha. [Aside:] My functions fail,
As though I were a fish who play'd the harp.   85
[To Cher:] Thou, Cher, art young and passing beautiful,
And I—

CHER   —And thou?

JOSH   —And I, um, er. Well . . . what?

CHER   Thou think'st me beautiful? Those were thy words,
         The few I heard amidst the gibbering.

JOSH   An ounce of beauty hast thou. Yea, or two.   90
         In faith, thou knowest thou art gorgeous, Cher—
         A face that would make Helen envious.
         Thou also art most popular, thy clique
         Surrounding thee an 'twere a swarm of bees,
         And thou the queen who sits as centerpiece.   95
         Yet—O! I almost did forget myself,
         For this—what quoth I of thy beauty rare—
         Is not the reason wherefore I have come
         Expending ev'ry day in working here.
         For I, who one day hopes to lawyer be,   100
         'Twas an experience profound and useful.

CHER   Those were thy words already, moments hence—
         If thou repeat'st thyself, learn not new lines,
         Another player may be call'd upon
         To act the part of lover, sighing like furnace.   105

JOSH   No other player seek, for I am he,
         Yet must remember why I hither came:
         Mel. I am here for Mel, for he alone
         Doth care about me in this ruthless world.

CHER   Nay, 'tis not so. Melodramatic be   110
         Thou not, and seek not others for this scene,
         For thy world doth contain abundant care—
         My father's not alone in loving thee.

JOSH   O, he is not?

CHER   —Nay.

JOSH   —Dare I one word more?
         Do thy words mean thou car'st for me as well?   115

CHER   More care have I than I could ever tell.

[They kiss joyfully. Exeunt.

SCENE 4

A wedding.

Enter BALTHASAR *on balcony.*

BALTHASAR   [*singing:*] Faithfully guarded, remain ye behind,
                 The blessing of love shall preserve you!

Triumphant courage, love, and happiness,
Connect under faith that shall serve you!
    You champion of youth, remain!   5
    You ornament of splendor, reign!
See now the splendors of the wedding feast,
And know you delights of the heart!
Sweet-smelling room, which was deck'd for romance,
Proclaimeth the strength of love's art!   10
    You champion of youth, &c.

Enter LADY TOBY GEIST *and* MASTER WENDELL HALL, *arrayed as
bride and groom, with their backs to the audience. Enter* MINISTER.
Enter CHER, *aside. Enter* DIONNE, TAI, JOSH, MURRAY, TRAVIS,
AMBER, LADY STOEGER, *and various* GUESTS *aside, seated.*

CHER   'Tis plain to see what would, thereafter, hap—
                Yet think ye not it is my nuptials!
                As if! As if I, but sixteen, would wed,
                As if it were Kentucky where I dwell,   15
                As if we quickly play'd the wedding bells,
                As if I ready were for such commitment.
MINISTER   Now wife and husband! Ye may gladly kiss.
                       [Lady Geist and Master Hall kiss.
                       All begin moving toward tables to sit.
TRAVIS   A stirring ceremony, truly.
TAI   Sweet Travis, paramour—thou art so right.   20
STOEGER   [*aside:*] How my mind serious and body strong
                Do love the romance of a wedding day!
TAI   [*to Dionne:*] When I have mine own wedding, some
                                     sweet day,
                A grand motif of flowers I desire,

	With garlands to surround my bridely frame—	25
DIONNE	Nay, nay. When I am wed, I plan to wear
	A sailor's dress—yet made to be a gown—
	My bridesmaids all adorn'd in sailors' hats.
MURRAY	[*to Travis and Josh:*] They plan our weddings far too

soon, methinks.

[*To the women:*] I pray, cease thy "'Til death do us

part" noise— 30

'Tis mumbo jumbo 'til we older are—
It fills my head with bugs.

JOSH   —Yea. Bugs. Me, too.

[*All laugh.*

STOEGER   Girls, quickly come—our Lady Geist shall throw
The nuptial bouquet, which doth portend
Who shall stand next upon the wedding dais.   35

[*Dionne and Tai follow her to where Lady
Geist prepares to throw the bouquet.*

JOSH   [*to Cher:*] We menfolk have a wager over who
Shall capture the bouquet when it is thrown—
Two hundred ducats is the current sum.

CHER   Leave it to me, my love—'tis mine in sooth.

[*Cher follows to where the
bouquet will be thrown.*

GEIST   Pray, gather ye around. 'Tis throwing time!   40

[*Lady Geist throws the bouquet, which Cher
initially catches. In confusion, all stumble
and fall together. Cher emerges with it.*

MURRAY   Are not our ladies humorous, my friends?

JOSH   Yea, and their loveliness knows naught of ends.

[*Cher returns to Josh and they
kiss. Exeunt omnes.*

EPILOGUE

Enter JANE, *a narrator.*

JANE   The wedding was like other weddings where
The parties have no taste for finery
Or crude parades. Yet, Amber—most unfair—
Declar'd it shabby unrefinedly.
In spite of these perceived deficiencies—   5
Too few lace veils, for satin small expense—
This counter'd all the insufficiencies:
The wishes, hopes, predictions, confidence
Of this small band of true friends who came nigh
To witness ceremony and communion,   10
Which all, in turn, were fully answer'd by
The perfect happiness of their sweet union.
Here is our end, conclusion, and finis—
In love, friends, may ye no more clueless be.

                                                [Exit.

END.

AFTERWORD

Could I write a Pop Shakespeare series and not include *Clueless*? As if!

I first saw *Clueless* sometime in the late '90s—if not in the theater, then shortly after. High school—which was formative for my love of Shakespeare—introduced me to Jane Austen; we read *Pride and Prejudice* in my junior year. As someone who has always been intrigued (this won't surprise you) by modern adaptations of the classics, *Clueless*—which is based on Austen's novel *Emma*—was right up my alley. Its enduring popularity makes it a great addition to the Pop Shakespeare series. (In preparation for writing this book, I watched *Clueless* and then read *Emma* for good measure.)

This is the first love story I've adapted, if by a love story we mean one that ends when lovers come together. The plot is probably closer to one Shakespeare might have created than any of my other books. Therefore, I decided early on that this book would be written as though it could take place in Shakespeare's time. Although *Clueless* contains cell phones, computers, cars, TVs, and so on, *William Shakespeare's The Taming of the Clueless* strips away the technology to leave a tale that could have been written in the 1600s. Mostly. There are still anachronisms—the characters talk about Jason Priestly, the mall, and Beverly Hills—but the setting is the turn of the seventeenth century. I confess that winding the clock backward on the story leads to a few odd moments. In the movie, after Cher is robbed she calls Josh from a pay phone; in my adaptation, he happens along just when she needs him.

I embellished the script of *Clueless* so that nearly every line has additional content and Shakespearean turns of phrase. As a result, this is my longest Shakespearean-style adaptation of a film, even though

Clueless is shorter than most movies I've adapted. Only one charac-
ter has a unique way of speaking; Travis, who is not known for his
smarts, has just nine syllables in each of his lines of iambic pentameter.
(Devoted readers know that I did the same thing with Jar Jar Binks.)
It bears mentioning that I also needed a Shakespearean equivalent
to the phrase "As if!" I made each "As if!" from the movie into an
anaphora, a device in which multiple lines start with the same words.

Two new characters appear in my adaptation. Balthasar—named
for the character of *Much Ado About Nothing* who sings "Sigh no
more, ladies"—provides the music. *Clueless* is the first movie I've
adapted that has a soundtrack composed almost entirely of popular
music, and the regular appearance of Balthasar is my way of featur-
ing the film's songs. Jane, the narrator who gives the prologue and
epilogue, is my nod to Jane Austen. Strangely, *William Shakespeare's
The Taming of the Clueless* is an adaptation of an adaptation, and as
a lifelong reader of Jane Austen I wanted to pay homage to the story's
original creator. Jane's words are adapted directly from the beginning
and end of *Emma*. (Of course, the wedding my epilogue mentions is
the marriage of Lady Geist and Master Hall, not that of Emma and
Mr. Knightley.)

Until next time, readers. I hope you enjoyed this merry detour into
the '90s.

The 1590s, that is.

⟩ ACKNOWLEDGMENTS ⟨

Thank you for being you: Jennifer Creswell, Liam Creswell, Graham Doescher, and J. Thomas.

Thank you for family: Bob and Beth Doescher, and Erik, Em, Aracelli, and Addison Doescher. Holly Havens, and Mona and Roland Havens. Jeff and Caryl Creswell, Joel Creswell, Sibyl Siegfried, and their daughter Sophie, and Katherine Creswell and Spencer Nietmann.

Thank you for friends: Josh Hicks, Alexis Kaushansky, and their daughter Ruby. Tom George and Kristin Gordon George. Apricot, David, Isaiah, and Oak Irving. Chloe Ackerman and Graham Steinke. Lucy Neary, Melody Burton, Jeannette Ehmke, Ali Wesley, and Jerryn Johnston. Heidi Altman and Scott Roehm, Chris and Andrea Martin, Naomi Walcott and Audu Besmer, and Ethan Youngerman and Rebecca Lessem. Emily, Josiah, and Bryony Carminati, Helga, Michael, Isabella, and Lottie Scott, and Ryan, Nicole, Mackinzie, Audrey and Lily Warne-McGraw. Travis Boeh and Sarah Woodburn, Chris Buehler and Marian Hammond, Erin and Nathan Buehler, Anne Huebsch, Tara and Michael Morrill, and Ben and Katie Wire. Steve Weeks and Dan Zehr. Kim Hoare, Callista and Geoff Isabelle, Ann, Daniel, Lewis, and Molly Orr, John Rohrs and Andie Wigodsky.

Thank you for my books: Jhanteigh Kupihea, Rebecca Gyllenhaal, Nicole De Jackmo, Ivy Weir, Jane Morley, Christina Schillaci, Kelsey Hoffman, Brett Cohen, Andie Reid, and everyone else.

Thank you for teachers and parent figures: Jane Bidwell, Doree Jarboe, Bruce McDonald, and Janice Morgan. Jim and Nancy Hicks, and Joan and Grady Miller.

Thank you for colleagues: Bernie Arnason, Mark Fordice, Jeremy Graves, and Dave Nieuwstraten. Giacomo Calabria and Farshad Farahat.

Thank you for hope: Antwon Chavis, Nate Housel, and K. Thomas.

Thank you for memories, and rest in peace: David Bartlett and Omid Nooshin.

READER'S GUIDE

You don't need to be a Shakespeare scholar to enjoy William Shakespeare's Taming of the Clueless. But if you've come to this book with more knowledge about the 1990s than the 1590s, or more experience dancing at the bar than studying scansion with the Bard, this reader's guide may help deepen your understanding of the language and structure of the book, all of which is inspired by Shakespeare's work.

The Language

Let's begin with the rhythm of Shakespeare's language, which is used throughout *William Shakespeare's Taming of the Clueless*, and which can be a difficult hurdle for new readers to jump. Shakespeare wrote his plays in a specific syllabic pattern known as iambic pentameter. An *iamb* is a unit of meter, sometimes called a foot, consisting of two syllables; the first is unstressed, or soft, and the second is stressed, or emphasized. An iamb sounds like "da-DUM," as beyond ("be-YOND"), across ("a-CROSS"), and Boleyn ("bo-LEYN"). *Pentameter* is a line of vers containing five feet. So iambic pentameter consists of five iambs, or ten syllables alternating in emphasis. A famous example of this meter, with the stressed half of each iamb in bold, is:

> I'd **rath**er **be** a **ham**mer **than** a **nail**.

However, as much as we associate Shakespeare with iambic pentameter, he broke the rule almost as often as he observed it. The most famous Shakespearean line all has eleven syllables, not ten: "To be or not to be, that is the question." That last *-ion* is known as a weak ending, or an unstressed syllable. Shakespeare often used weak endings, added two unstressed syllables where there should be one, and left out syllables entirely.

Let's see iambic pentameter in action with this speech from Act V, scene 1 (see pages 157–158).

MEL	Unless thou hast into a vulture turn'd—	35
	Which paceth to and fro and back and forth	
	Until a living animal hath turn'd	
	To carrion that sates the appetite—	
	Thou shouldst not tut about like one who waits.	
	Hast thou some matter burning in thy heart	40
	That causeth thee to fret and sigh and groan?	
	Why dost thou dance athwart my office door	
	As if thou had some issue to discuss	
	Yet wert afraid to bring the matter forth?	

Mel's speech follows the rules of iambic pentameter. I hear the rhythm most clearly in line 41: "That **causeth thee** to **fret** and **sigh** and **groan**?"

If you read this speech aloud, you may notice that the dialogue sounds unnatural if spoken according to how the individual lines are broken. Rather, punctuation should guide how lines of iambic pentameter are spoken, as if the speech were written as prose. Consider lines 35–39: "Unless thou hast into a vulture turn'd— / Which paceth to and fro and back and forth / Until a living animal hath turn'd / To carrion that sates the appetite— / Thou shouldst not tut about like one who waits." This single sentence is split across five lines. When read aloud, each line that ends with no punctuation should roll into the next line.

What about words with more than two syllables? The trick with multisyllabic words is to figure out which syllable has the primary emphasis, and then see if another syllable has a minor emphasis. The word *intelligent* is a good example. The primary emphasis is on the second syllable, int**ell**igent. In iambic pentameter, it makes sense to pronounce it as two iambs, "int**ell**-" and the next iamb to be "-**igent**." The final syllable *-gent* has a secondary stress that fits the meter nicely.

To Thee or Not to Thee?

Shakespeare's work is well known to be full of archaic pronouns (think thee and thou) and verbs ending in *-est* and *-eth* that can sound jarring to a modern ear. Consider this your crash course in these unfamiliar terms.

- **thou:** second person singular pronoun that's the subject of a sentence, as in "thou hast." Modern writers would use *you*.
- **thee:** second person singular pronoun that's the object of a sentence, as in "that causeth thee to fret." Modern writers would use *you*.
- **ye:** second person plural pronoun that's either the subject or object of a sentence. Modern writers would use *you*.
- **thy:** second person singular possessive before a word starting with a consonant, as in "thy head." Modern writers would use *your*.
- **thine:** second person singular possessive before a word starting with a vowel, as in "thine assistance." Modern writers would use *your*.

In Shakespeare's time, the pronoun *you* was used either as the second person plural or as the second person singular in formal settings. For example, a citizen would generally call the king *you*, not *thou* (which, in fact, might be considered an insult).

In general, the *-est* ending (sometimes shortened, with an apostrophe, to *-st* or just *-t*) is added to a verb whose subject is the pronoun *thou*: "thou hast" or "thou shouldst." The *-eth* ending accompanies verbs whose subject is *he*, *she*, or a singular *it*. For example, when referring to the vulture, Mel says "Which paceth to and fro back and forth."

Another note about verb endings: In Shakespeare's time, the *-ed* at the end of a past tense verb was sometimes pronounced as a separate syllable. Whereas a modern speaker would pronounce the word *turned* as one syllable, back then people would have pronounced two syllables: "turn-ed." When such a word needed to be shortened to fit the meter, Shakespeare wrote it as a contraction: *turn'd*. In modern editions of Shakespeare—and in William Shakespeare's *Taming of the Clueless*—an accent over the e indicates that the *-ed* should be pronounced as a separate syllable: *turnèd*.

Other Shakespearean Hallmarks

The following features of Shakespeare's plays can all be found in *William Shakespeare's Taming of the Clueless*.

- **Five acts.** This was the usual structure of plays in Shakespeare's time, which drew on the earlier tradition of ancient Roman plays. Acts can contain any number of scenes.

- **Minimal stage directions.** Shakespeare left it to the performers to determine who should do what on stage, offering only minimal guidance on the page. I tried to do the same when writing *William Shakespeare's Taming of the Clueless*, though it has far more stage directions than a Shakespearean play would, to make action sequences clear.
- **Rhyming couplets at the end of scenes.** A rhyming couplet is a pair of consecutive lines of verse that rhyme. For example, Act I, scene 3, lines 139–140 (see page 33): "Though we awhile may see each other more, / Unto thy heart to her ope not the door." Shakespeare ended his scenes this way to mark a narrative shift, similar to a final cadence in music.
- **Asides.** An aside is dialogue that the audience can hear but that the characters other than the speaker (supposedly) do not. These speeches often explain a character's motivations or inner thoughts or reveal background information to the audience. These days, an aside in theater is sometimes called "breaking the fourth wall," that is, crossing the imaginary divide between stage and audience to address the spectators directly.
- **Soliloquies.** These monologues are similar to asides in that they explain a character's behavior or motivation. But they occur when the character is alone on stage and tend to be longer than asides.

Literary Devices

Throughout *William Shakespeare's Taming of the Clueless*, I made direct references to lines from Shakespeare's plays. (How many did you find?) In addition, I also borrowed the following Shakespearean literary devices.

- **Anaphora.** Anaphora is the repetition of a word or phrase at the start of successive lines, used for rhetorical effect. One example from Shakespeare appears in Act II, scene 4, lines 11–15 of *The First Part of Henry the Sixth*. I used this device in *William Shakespeare's Taming of the Clueless* every time a character utters the phrase "As if!" The following example is from Act I, scene 1, lines 196–199 (see page 22):

> CHER   As if he should so blatantly approach,
>
> As if I would, then, fall into his arms,
>
> As if we two familiar would become,
>
> As if he could usurp my maidenhood!

- **Extended wordplay.** Shakespeare drew multiple meanings from words and squeezed as much life from them as possible. One excellent example of Shakespearean wordplay occurs in Act II, scene 1, of *The Taming of the Shrew*, when Kate and Petruchio verbally spar in one of their first scenes together. I wrote a similar interaction—including Petruchio's line "With my tongue in your tail?"—when Cher and Josh first appear together in *William Shakespeare's Taming of the Clueless* in Act I, scene 2, lines 22–38 (see page 29). See how many plays on words (either the same word or homonym pairs) you can find in the following passage.

> JOSH   Holla, my halfway sister. Thou art here,
>
> So who then watcheth o'er the Galléria,
>
> Where thou dost ever spend thy precious time?
>
> CHER   Thy shirt of flannel—dost thou pay respect   25
>
> Unto the gods who make Seattle gray,
>
> Or merely, mayhap, needest thou the warmth
>
> Because thou near the ice house ever stand'st?

JOSH	Thy belly filleth like a burlap sack.
CHER	Thy face doth race to catch up with thy mouth, 30
	For both are filthy.
JOSH	—If thou wouldst face truth,
	Thy tongue is far too sharp to match thy mien.
CHER	Thy face too mean for me to hold my tongue.
JOSH	Thy sharpness tells a tale a man could fear.
CHER	Thy tongue and face should turn their tails and
	flee. 35
JOSH	A flea would gladly take a turn on thee.
CHER	Thy tongue dost turn its face to tales. Farewell.
JOSH	With my tongue in your tail? Let us restart.

- **Songs.** Shakespeare's plays are full of songs. Sometimes playful, sometimes mystical, sometimes sorrowful, songs appear at unexpected moments and often break the rhythm of iambic pentameter. I adapted several tunes from the *Clueless* soundtrack for this play. Here's my adaptation of the film's most famous song, from Act II, scene 4, lines 108–118 (see page 79).

BALTHASAR	[*singing:*] 'Tis Saturday, and I do roll,
	My homies near, my spirit full,
	Some sixteen instruments do play, 110
	Unto the shore we make our way!
	Roll with the homies, saucy jack!
	Roll with the homies, sip the yak!
	My carriage is a hearty ride,
	The people gawk when I'm outside, 115
	No gang of rogues our joy reduce—
	My homies bear the dinner juice.
	Roll with the homies, &c.

SONNET 1995

The Internet in '95? As if!

The lovers Cher and Josh have been united,
Our tale of love and cluelessness concludes.
We hope our story hath thine eyes delighted,
For we would bring thee future interludes.
If there is more that thou desirest still,
Quirkbooks.com should be thy destination.
Pop Shakespeare titles shall bring thee a thrill
Should thy heart need a further palpitation.
If thou wouldst know more of the author's mind,
The website ever is the place to be!
An **interview with Ian Doescher** find,
He'll answer all thy questions ardently.
Be thou not clueless, nay, but ere the dawn,
Hie to Quirk Books, be calm, and carry on!

quirkbooks.com/tamingoftheclueless